BEHOLD the birds of the air:
They neither sow or reap,
        nor gather into barns,
And yet your heavenly
        Father feeds them.

Matthew 6: 26

GOD gives to every bird
its proper food,
but they must all
        fly for it.

Old Proverb

Blackbird

Male

Red-Winged Blackbird

The Red-winged Blackbird is one of the most common birds in the U.S. and is found in every state. Its most striking feature is the colorful red patch on the wing of the male which appears when the bird is excited. At other times, this patch is mostly concealed by black feathers with only a yellow fringe visible. This patch is called an "epaulet" by ornithologists (from the French word "*epaulette*," meaning a type of shoulder ornament on a military uniform).

During the breeding season in spring and summer, the Red-winged Blackbird takes up a position atop a tall bush or cattail and spends most of each day defending its territory.

The Red-winged Blackbird makes a loud and distinctive "*chuck*" or "*check*" sound when disturbed. The "*oka-lee*" song is one of the first sounds of spring.

Other blackbirds include cowbirds and grackles, but not crows or starlings (although they are black, they belong to different families).

Like a Window Shade

When the Red-winged Blackbird gets amorously or aggressively excited, small muscles raise a few black feathers revealing bright red feathers underneath. The red patches show the bird's alarm upon discovering an intruder on its territory. They are also displayed as part of courtship in spring. Researchers covered the red patches of selected males and found that the poor birds soon lost their territories and for this reason, were unable to attract mates.

This photo shows the patch partially covered. The breeding season is over and the red feathers have molted, leaving only dull orange feathers.

Because of its very prominent and fascinating red patch, many people call this bird a "red-wing," although its entire wing is not red.

Female at nest

Unanimous Consent

Blackbird flocks may consist of a few individuals or enough birds to blacken the sky. The truly large flocks may number in the millions. In any case, they seem to make all decisions, such as where to feed, without any bickering and without any apparent leader. How such decisions are made remains a very intriguing mystery. It is this mutual agreement that makes flocking possible. By remaining together in flocks, individual birds benefit from the large number of eyes that constantly keep watch for predators.

Foraging Flocks

During fall and winter, Red-wings form "mixed-foraging flocks" with other blackbirds. During this period they are not territorial but range over wide areas, swooping down into fields to gobble up all the food in sight before moving elsewhere. Flocking is so basic to the Red-wing that it was given the Latin genus name, Agelaius, meaning "belonging to a flock."

△ The spreading of the tail feathers by this female is called a "song-spread display." It is a threat used to defend territory (primarily against other females of her own species).

△ The female is strikingly different from the male in shape and color and is easily mistaken for a large sparrow. If there is a surplus of females, Red-winged Blackbirds are sometimes polygynous. One male may establish nests with several different females.

Bluebird

Eastern Bluebird

This lovely creature is called the "bluebird of happiness" because of its wonderful color and beautiful song and also because its arrival in the northern states announces the beginning of spring. It is a quiet, gentle bird, never raucous like jays or some of the other backyard favorites.

The blue color is truly intense. The American philosopher Henry David Thoreau, a great admirer of the bluebird, wrote that this bird "carries the sky on its back."

The Pilgrims are said to have called it the "blue robin" in homage to one of the best-loved European birds. There is an Indian legend that this bird was once a dull color, but because of its gentleness, the gods allowed it to bathe in a sacred lake of incredibly blue water, and the bluebird emerged from the bath with its striking plumage.

The bluebird, like the robin, is a member of the thrush family. Although its brilliant color bears no resemblance to the colors of the more familiar thrushes, the nestling bluebirds are heavily speckled on their breasts just like baby thrushes.

The bluebird is not a backyard bird. Since it eats mostly insects, it is not attracted to feeders. It can be seen sitting on fence posts around open fields, especially fields at the edges of pine woods, pastures, and orchards.

Male

Female

A few bluebirds remain in the Northeast all winter, especially along the coast, and can be attracted to a feeder during very cold weather.

How Birds Perch Safely on Power Lines

Electric current will not flow from a power line unless the wire makes a connection with a "ground." Insulators prevent power lines from touching metal support poles, so the flow of electricity continues along the wires without traveling to the ground.

Since a bird's body is not as good a conductor as a wire, electricity will not flow through its body when it perches on a power line but will take the easier route through the wire without harming the bird. However, if a bird touches a wire and a pole at the same time, it will complete the connection with the ground, and the bird may be electrocuted.

The Nesting Box Program

Bluebirds nest in holes in trees or fence posts. They are under pressure from the starlings and house sparrows for nesting space. Bluebird lovers have organized to provide specially designed nesting boxes to insure that their population does not decline.

In addition to loss of habitat and competition from starlings and sparrows, the bluebird must compete against the very aggressive Tree Swallow for nest holes. Fortunately, one Tree Swallow will not permit another Tree Swallow to nest nearby. So, if there are two nest holes close together and one is occupied by a Tree Swallow, the other may be used by a bluebird without fear. The neighboring Tree Swallow will keep all other Tree Swallows a safe distance away. For this reason, bluebird nest boxes are frequently set out in pairs, one for the swallow and one for the bluebird.

There is a Bluebird Society which promotes nest box programs and has established many bluebird nesting trails, which are lines of nest boxes, often placed at intervals along highways or back roads. Such trails require regular maintenance, but these trails have done much to help restore bluebird populations.

Wooden lid

This drawing shows a simple way to construct a bluebird nest box by drilling a cavity in a fence post and adding a lid. An opening of $1\frac{1}{2}$ inches admits a bluebird but is too small for a starling.

WG/Vireo

WB/VU

◁ This pair of bluebirds are attempting to chase starling intruders away from their nest box. Although they appear to be winning this confrontation, this is not the usual case. Nest boxes or natural nest sites are often occupied by starlings prior to the arrival of the bluebirds in spring, and in most cases, the birds that are in a nest first can successfully defend it against intruders.

◁ A typical trail of bluebird nest boxes.

BB

Bobolink

Bobolink

The male Bobolink is a bird many authors describe as having a tuxedo on backwards, with the black in front and the white in back. It is the only North American land bird which is mostly white above and dark below.

Bobolinks winter in South America and arrive in the Northeast in May. In open, grassy fields they can be found nesting on the ground in widely spread colonies consisting of a dozen or more pairs. They often become the victims of mechanized hay mowers, one of the sad results of modern farming. The old-style farmer with a scythe could easily avoid the nests.

Bobolinks eat the seeds of wild grasses and the insects associated with the grasslands. They also favor grains, especially rice. Although the Bobolink is considered an economically valuable bird in the Northeast for its consumption of insects, in earlier times, when rice plantations were common in the Carolinas and Georgia, it was a plague to the rice farmers of those states during its migrations, and it was even called the "rice-bird," a name usually preceded by a curse.

Male

Female

△ Only the upper back is black. The lower back and rump are white, as are two patches on either side of the upper back above the wings. Note also the yellow patch on the back of the neck (which can be raised during courtship displays).

◁ Bobolinks are known for their impressive songs which are complex and consist of many notes.

Bobwhite

Common Bobwhite

This bird says its name. The call is a very clear "Bob-WHITE!!"

The bobwhite is a gamebird and can be legally hunted in many states during limited hunting seasons. A ground dweller, it is commonly seen in pine forests. Hikers will frequently flush whole families which run from one hiding place to another. If really threatened, one of the parents may try to distract an intruder by running into an open clearing while its family disperses in the underbrush.

At the end of the breeding season, several bobwhite families may band together to form small flocks called "coveys." Their members benefit from the protection of greater numbers.

When families of bobwhite roost for the night, they cluster together in a

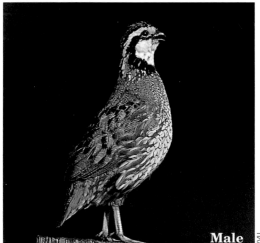

Male

Female

circle, facing outward with their bodies touching. This "wagon-train" formation helps conserve warmth and allows them to watch for predators in all directions.

The bobwhite is now seldom encountered in New York and New England. Its decline has been attributed to abandoned farming, reforestation, over-hunting, and heavy winter mortality. Efforts persist to restock the area with hardy genetic varieties from the upper Midwest.

The most obvious features of the bobwhite are the small head and plump body. The adult male has a white throat and a white stripe above the eye. In the female, these areas are brownish.

Buntings

Indigo Bunting

Buntings are small-billed finches. They are relatives of cardinals and sparrows and are rather shy birds. They rarely come to feeders. They feel more comfortable if there is plenty of underbrush available so they can quickly hide if threatened.

The name "bunting" may come from the German word "bunt," meaning "speckled." Some species of buntings are speckled, but none of the North American species have speckled or mottled plumage.

The male Indigo Bunting sings its territorial songs from perches in open places, including utility lines and isolated trees. It nests commonly throughout the Northeast in brushy fields and the edges of woodlands.

Note that the male Indigo Bunting is blue all over, while the Eastern Bluebird is only blue on its back and wings.

Male Indigo Bunting

Snow Bunting

Snow Buntings nest further north than any other bird (the northern tip of Greenland). In winter, they appear in the Northeast in flocks. Along with the juncos, they are the "snowbirds," birds which are often seen when snow is on the ground.

Male in breeding plumage

Winter plumage

Cardinal

Male

Northern Cardinal

The cardinal may have been named for the way the brilliant plumage of the male resembles the scarlet robes worn by cardinals of the Roman Catholic Church. The crest of feathers on the head and the jet-black mask on the face help make the cardinal one of the most spectacular of all the backyard birds.

The female cardinal does all the nest-building. The male often brings her food and feeds her so she doesn't have to stop working until the nest is completed.

Cardinals are very territorial and will chase other birds away from a feeder. They are also known for their attacks against windows which reflect their own images. The attacking cardinal imagines that the reflected image is another cardinal invading his territory. There are several ways of discouraging such attacks. Try soaping the window so it is not so reflective. Other possibilities include hanging an owl image in the window or putting a rubber snake on the sill. If nothing is done, the attacks might continue throughout the nesting season.

Both males and females have a large, distinctive, pointed crest on the tops of their heads. The crest is raised when the birds are alarmed.

Female

Cardinals love sunflower seeds and will find them and pick them out if a variety of seeds is offered at a feeder. Their heavy, powerful bills are very effective for cracking the hard shells. Although the adults eat both seeds and insects, baby cardinals are fed insects by their parents.

Cardinals are very "romantic" birds, at least during the breeding season in the spring. They are usually seen in pairs and have an extensive variety of courtship rituals. The male often offers bits of food to the female during courtship. At other times of the year the male may be indifferent, and he may even drive the female away from a feeder. But, during the spring, the pair will become very close. The male may stretch his neck and raise his crest as he sings.

Rare albino cardinal

Birds Feeding Fish

A cardinal was observed feeding a goldfish at an outdoor pond. One possible explanation is that when the goldfish came to the surface to gulp air as they commonly do, the breeding cardinal was stimulated to feed this open mouth as if it was a young cardinal begging for food.

The All-Time Champion "State Bird"

The cardinal is the official state bird of seven states: Illinois, Indiana, Kentucky, North Carolina, Ohio, Virginia, and West Virginia. No other bird can claim as much official recognition, but the Western Meadowlark comes close with six states.

The Advance of the Cardinal

In the early part of this century, the cardinal was strictly a southern bird. Now, its range extends well into Canada. There are a number of theories which attempt to explain this dramatic expansion northward.

One theory credits the general warming of the climate during this century. Another theory cites the increase in human population, which creates new trails of bird feeders. This extra food supply might allow cardinals to survive in areas which were previously marginal.

Catbird

Gray Catbird

This almost entirely gray bird is best known for its "mewing" cat-like call, most frequently heard when the bird is disturbed. It has a range of more musical songs which it sings when it is courting or advertising its territory to other males. It is also a skilled mimic of other birds. This is not surprising, since the catbird is a close relative of the mockingbird.

The catbird usually stays hidden in heavy brush, but it loves to bathe and can be attracted to a garden with a bird bath.

The top photo shows the distinctive black marking on the top of the catbird's head which birders call a "cap." There are also chestnut colored feathers under the tail which are often not noticed. If you are looking for exciting color, try another species.

Catbirds will not eat seed at a feeder unless it has been softened through exposure to the weather. They can be more easily attracted with raisins.

A Shortcut for Suet

Almost all the birds that come to feeders will eat suet (hard animal fat from the area of the loins and kidneys). Beef kidney fat is best. Although it will turn black on the edges, it will not spoil and become rancid as quickly as other fats.

Here is an easy way to provide fat for birds. Combine 1 cup of bacon drippings, 1 cup of corn meal, $1/2$ cup of flour, 1 cup of water, and 1 tablespoon of sugar. Mix together and cook for five minutes. Mixed bird seed can be added. Shape into "muffins" on a cookie sheet and freeze. Store in plastic bags in the freezer.

Land birds do not have adequate mechanisms to remove salt from their bodies, so salty fats like bacon grease are not good for them unless they are mixed with something else. The same goes for peanuts. Raw peanuts are okay, but salted peanuts may be harmful.

Care of Orphan Birds

When a baby bird has fallen from its nest, it is best to place the bird back in the nest if possible. It is not true that parents will reject a baby that has been handled by humans. If the nest has been destroyed or cannot be found, create a new nest with a hanging basket and some grass.

If a baby bird is well feathered and can hop around and fly a little, place him in some bushes away from predators. He may have left the nest a day or two before the usual time for fledging. Bird parents force their young out of the nest as soon as possible, because nests are easily located by predators such as snakes, squirrels, jays, and crows. The longer a baby bird stays in the nest after it is capable of leaving, the less its chances for survival.

If the parents do not return within five or six hours, you may decide the baby needs further care. Unfeathered babies can be placed in a box with a heating pad on a low setting (do not cook the bird!). Feathered babies do not need heat and can be placed on paper towels. An emergency formula can be made by mashing hard-boiled egg yolks with a little warm water and administering the mixture with an eye dropper when the baby calls for food.

Some birds, especially baby mockingbirds, must have vitamins or they quickly become so weak they cannot perch. Bird vitamins are available at pet shops.

If possible, contact your local wildlife rehabilitation center. Keeping wild birds is against the law. A person whose true purpose is to keep a colorful songster as a pet cage bird can always use the excuse that he was only helping a sick or orphaned bird. Wildlife officers might be strict about enforcing the law if they suspect such a situation.

Chickadee

Black-capped Chickadee

The chickadee says its name when it calls *"chick-a-dee-dee-dee."* The Black-capped Chickadee has little trouble making a living from insects, even during winter, but it is nonetheless one of the most enthusiastic visitors to backyard feeders. It can become tame enough to be hand-fed. A very acrobatic bird, it has no trouble using hanging feeders and is especially fond of sunflower seeds.

Chickadees have orderly social relations, with a dominant pair the leaders of a flock. Dominance is shown through several displays. A slight puffing of the feathers of the black cap causes most subordinate birds to back off. If this is not sufficient, the entire plumage may be puffed out.

During the breeding season, the dominant pair will have its choice of territories and that may include a feeder. So if your feeder welcomed a whole flock of chickadees in winter, it will likely serve only two from spring until early fall. After breeding is complete, the chickadees join together again to form foraging flocks for the winter.

Except during the breeding season, chickadees travel in bands of various small birds which may include titmice, nuthatches, kinglets, creepers, and Downy Woodpeckers.

Notice the markings of the Black-capped Chickadee, which are described as "a black cap and a bib."

South of New York City, the Black-capped Chickadee range starts to overlap that of the Carolina Chickadee, but it takes an expert to tell the difference between these two birds.

Chickadee Mosaic

Nationwide, there are seven different chickadee species and their ranges are quite clearly defined (although there is some overlapping). These separate ranges illustrate a principle of ecology which states that two species with the same habitat requirements generally cannot coexist. One will finally prevail over the other in a certain area.

Black-capped Chickadee

Boreal Chickadee

◁ In northern New England and Canada, there is also a brownish chickadee species called the Boreal Chickadee. The Boreal prefers spruce-evergreen forests, in contrast to the Black-capped which can accept a variety of habitats. This means that the birder must go out into the woods to find a Boreal Chickadee.

Cowbird

Male

Brown-headed Cowbird

Cowbirds follow cattle around pastures in the same manner as Cattle Egrets and get their name from this close association with cows. The movement of the big animals stirs up insects in the grass which the cowbirds catch. They are especially fond of grasshoppers.

The female cowbird wears gray plumage, unlike its mate. This strong male-female difference is a common characteristic of many blackbird species, including the Red-winged Blackbird and the grackles.

Female

Baby cowbird screaming for attention

Ungrateful Stepchildren

The baby cow-birds do not follow the habits of their foster parents but join other cowbirds shortly after they leave the nest.

Cowbird chick being fed by its foster parent, a Blue-winged Warbler.

The Foster Parent Plan

The cowbird is a "nest parasite." It lays its eggs in the nests of other birds. Cardinals are common victims, as are Red-winged Blackbirds and many species of warblers. The cowbird is the only land bird in the United States with this trait. There are a few ducks that parasitize nests, and it is a common behavior among cuckoos in many other parts of the world.

Most of the birds chosen as foster parents will tolerate the extra egg and treat the hatchling as one of their own. However, cowbird eggs hatch quickly, and the baby cowbird frequently out-grows and out-eats the offspring of the host birds. The cowbird chick is often the only survivor.

Not all birds will accept a cowbird egg laid in their nest. The response varies with the species. Some species will remove the egg, some will abandon or rebuild the nest, and some will even build another nest layer right on top of the cowbird egg.

Creeper

Brown Creeper

Streaked brown plumage enables this bird to disappear against the bark of trees. The Brown Creeper creeps up tree trunks, starting at the bottom and working toward the top, straight up or more likely, in a spiral, probing for insects with its long, curved beak.

The Brown Creeper uses its delicate, thin beak to poke into crevices. It cannot dig into bark in the same manner as woodpeckers which possess sturdy chisel-beaks. However, like the woodpeckers, the Brown Creeper does use its stiff tail for support.

The Brown Creeper builds a hammock-shaped nest of mosses, spider webs, and small twigs tucked under a strip of bark against the trunk of a dead tree.

No Looking Back

Upon reaching the top of one tree, the Brown Creeper flies to the bottom of another tree to continue its search for insects and larvae. It seldom climbs downward, if at all. This is in contrast to the nuthatch, which starts at the top of a tree and works its way down headfirst.

Crossbills

Red Crossbill, White-winged Crossbill

The most obvious characteristic of this bird is its crossed mandibles. This uniquely designed bill is used to pry open pine cones so that the crossbill can remove the pine seeds with its tongue.
▷ Close-up showing details of the bill of the Red Crossbill. This bird is molting its feathers.

Red Crossbill

White-winged Crossbill

The Legend of the Crossbill

There is a legend that the crossbill twisted its beak while trying to remove the nails from the hands of Jesus when He was on the cross. A similar legend is that the robin's breast was stained red with the blood of Christ as it tried to pull the thorns from His crown. Neither the crossbill nor the robin is mentioned in the biblical account of the execution of Christ, and these legends apparently developed later. The only bird mentioned in the Gospels is the cock which crowed when Peter denied his Master.

Crows

**American Crow
Fish Crow**

Not Blackbirds

Although black in color, crows are not blackbirds. They belong to a different family from the true blackbirds. In the Northeast, the true blackbirds are Red-winged Blackbirds, grackles, and cowbirds. Crows belong to the same family as jays and ravens.

Two Kinds (But You Might Not Notice)

There are two species of crows in the Northeast, the American Crow (also called the Common Crow) and the Fish Crow. Even experts cannot always tell the two apart visually. The Fish Crow is usually found in coastal areas and around fresh water while the Common Crow prefers drier places. The range of the Fish Crow does not extend north of eastern Massachusetts.

Different Voices

The two crows can be identified by their voices. The "caw" sound of the Fish Crow is slightly different from that of the American Crow. It is rather nasal and sounds more like "cah" or "uh-uh." Fish Crows and American Crows do not usually mix, so within a flock of crows, most likely all the birds will be of the same species. Experts identify them mostly by the sound of their calls.

Really Smart

The crow family may contain the most highly evolved birds in terms of intelligence. The cleverness of crows is legendary. This intelligence is put to use in foraging for food. The curious crow will investigate any possible source of food, such as a discarded sandwich inside a plastic wrapper. A crow would be more likely to figure out how to remove the wrapper than any other bird. Crows store food in inconspicuous places whenever there is a surplus available, and they try to keep the caches hidden by covering them with any available materials.

Lovable Birds?

In spite of their bold, blustering ways, crows have many endearing characteristics, at least in human terms. Most crows mate for life. They look after their offspring longer than most other birds, training them until they have learned all the wily ways necessary to succeed as a crow. They are extremely loyal, and the whole flock often comes to the aid of a wounded crow. Recordings of crow distress calls have been used by hunters to lure and slaughter large numbers of crows. The crow can make a wide range of sounds in addition to the well known "caw." Thanks to this ability, pet crows can be trained to talk quite well.

△ Crows have feathers extending down over their beaks and covering their nostrils.

Cuckoos

Yellow-billed Cuckoo

Black-billed Cuckoo
Yellow-billed Cuckoo

The use of the word "cuckoo" to indicate craziness possibly relates to the silly behavior of the little birds in cuckoo clocks. It may also derive from the repetitiousness of the cuckoo's call.

The Yellow-billed Cuckoo has a noticeable yellow coloring in the lower part of its beak. Its breast is pure white.

Cuckoos are known to sing more often on very humid days. High humidity often precedes rain, and so began the legend that the song of the cuckoo can be used to predict rain. For this reason, cuckoos have been called "rain crows."

European cuckoos are the species which say their name, but North American cuckoos do not have the cuckoo call. Instead, their call is a series of clicks. The Yellow-billed Cuckoo's call is easily immitated by rapid clicking tapering to slower clicks at the end.

▷ An interesting and attractive feature of the Yellow- billed Cuckoo is that it has feathers extending down its legs. Note that the leg itself is not feathered.

Black-billed Cuckoo

European and American cuckoos are different in their "family" behaviors. New World cuckoos lay eggs in their own nests and raise their own young. Old World cuckoos parisitize the nests of other birds the same as our Brown-headed Cowbird. This behavior is the basis for the term "cuckold" which refers to one man's wife bearing another man's child.

Doves

Rock Dove

This is the domestic pigeon commonly seen in parks. A native of Europe and Asia (where it is still a wild species) it was introduced to this continent hundreds of years ago. Varieties of this bird are very popular for racing, especially in Europe. The Rock Dove shows many variations of plumage.

In the United States, the Rock Dove is usually seen in cities, where it has found ways to coexist with man and has made a nuisance of itself in many places. The Rock Doves in cities have become very tame and will eat from your hand. However, Rock Doves found outside of cities are just as wild as other birds.

Doves can suck up water while bending their heads downward. Most birds don't have this ability and must use their beaks to scoop up water and then tilt their heads back in order to swallow.

△ This Rock Dove is sunbathing on a roof. Birds frequently spread their wings to "catch some rays" but not in quest of the perfect tan. More likely, it gives some relief from feather mites. Spreading the wings may cause the mites to move to the shady underside of the wings, where they can be more easily removed by preening.

Doves

Mourning Dove

Symbols of Peace and Glad Tidings

Doves are known as symbols of peace. In the Bible, Noah received an olive branch from the beak of a dove. Solomon spoke of the joyful time "when the voice of the turtle is heard in the land," referring to the cry of the turtle-dove. In Christianity, the Lord is sometimes referred to as the "heavenly dove." "Lo, the heavens were opened unto him and he saw the Spirit of God descending like a dove..." (Matthew 3:16)

In Islamic regions, the courtyards surrounding mosques often host large flocks of doves. The doves are treated with great respect, because it is written that Allah communicated some of his wisdom to Mohammed using a dove as the messenger.

A Cranky Bird?

The use of the dove as a symbol of peace and love is somewhat misleading. Although doves look like gentle birds, people with feeders know that the Mourning Dove is very feisty and is always squabbling with other birds.

Doves Vs. Pigeons

Doves and pigeons belong to the same family and the names are often used interchangeably. Both male and female birds can feed their young "pigeon's milk," which is not really milk. It is a sloughed-off layer of skin tissue from the bird's crop plus whatever food is in the crop (usually a mixture of finely ground and partially digested seeds).

The Mourning Dove is one of the most common and popular backyard birds. The soft "cooing" sound of this bird is most frequently heard early in the morning, often before sunrise. Because of this early morning activity, this bird is often mistakenly called the "morning dove."

Many people mistake the "cooing" for the voice of an owl. The Mourning Dove was apparently given its name by someone who considered its call mournful, but many people find the sound soothing and delightful.

Notice that the Mourning Dove bobs its head as it walks and makes a loud whistling noise with its wings while in flight.

Mourning Doves breed throughout the continental United States and are the target of many hunters. Dove hunting is considered an important tradition in many parts of the country.

When it comes to building a nest, the Mourning Dove is notoriously sloppy and will make do with almost any little pile of sticks. Sometimes Mourning Doves will dispense with nest construction altogether

and simply use the remains of another bird's nest, adding a few bits and pieces of their own. Mourning Doves have been known to lay eggs right on the ground or in the crotches of tree branches with no nest at all.

▷ During the breeding season, in the spring, the male Mourning Dove has a patch of iridescent color on each side of its neck. Throughout this period, the coloring of the beautiful blue eye-ring and bright orange legs is much more intense.

Baby Mourning Dove "puffing" feathers for extra insulation against the cold.

Finches

American Goldfinch

Goldfinches breed in the northern states during late summer. They use thistle-down in building their nests and also eat the thistle seeds. Since the northern thistles develop late in the season, the goldfinch is one of the last spring migrants to arrive after wintering in the south, and it does not build its nest until July.

No Gold in Winter

The American Goldfinch is famous for the brilliant color of the male, but after the breeding season has ended, goldfinches and other migrants molt and lose their brilliant feathers. On their way south in the fall, these birds are rather drab and identification *becomes difficult. Birders call them "LBJ's" or Little Brown Jobs. Fortunately, these same birds have their most brilliant plumage when they arrive again in the spring to breed. If the winter remains mild, some goldfinches may remain around feeding stations in the Northeast.*

Gathering thistle-down

The Finch Family

The birds in this book are organized alphabetically by common name. This makes reference easy for readers with little scientific knowledge of birds. But in a strictly scientific publication or a field guide, birds would be grouped together by families. The finch family includes a number of common birds that the untrained bird-lover might not realize are closely related. Cardinals, grosbeaks, and buntings are all members of this family. As finches, they all have heavy, seed-cracking beaks. But these birds do not share a common color. In fact, their colors span the entire color wheel, including all the primary colors: red, yellow and blue.

Here too there can be confusion between the standard common names of birds and their local names. While the cardinal is often referred to as the "redbird" without confusion, it is more likely to cause a problem when a Blue Grosbeak or an Indigo Bunting is locally referred to as a "blue bird." A novice could easily be confused into thinking he had found the Eastern Bluebird, a different bird completely unrelated to finches.

House Finch

The House Finch is a native of the Pacific Coast which was introduced in the East and now is well established along the Atlantic Coast as far north as Maine.

Male House Finch
(winter plumage)

Male and Female House Finches

Purple Finch

The Purple Finch brightens a winter day in the Northeast when it visits feeding stations during winter. It is much less common now than it was 40 years ago.

House Finch -vs- Purple Finch

Although these two species seem very similar and may often appear together on bird feeders, there are several field marks which help to tell them apart. Note that the House Finch has brown stripes on its sides and belly, and that in many cases its reddish head is more intensely colored than that of the male Purple Finch. To identify the very similar females, note that the female Purple Finch has a whitish eyebrow and dark ear patch whereas the female House Finch has a more even-toned, light-colored face.

Male Purple Finch

Male

Female

Flycatchers

Great Crested Flycatcher

Introduction to Flycatchers

Flycatchers spend much of the day perched on branches, waiting for insect prey. When an insect appears, they sally forth to catch it in flight. Since they spend much of their time in the tops of trees where they are difficult to see, birders usually locate them by their calls. As insect eaters, they are not drawn to backyard feeders, but can be attracted with drinking water.

Flycatcher populations are declining because of the destruction of rain forests in Central and South America. These rain forests are home to flycatchers in winter.

Great Crested Flycatcher

The Great Crested belongs to a group of flycatchers called *Myiarchus* which, except for the Great Crested, consists of tropical birds. The Great Crested is the only *Myiarchus* flycatcher found in the eastern U.S. This olive-brown bird with a gray throat is easily identified by two features of the *Myiarchus* group: a yellow belly and rusty-brown tail. Birders frequently spot the Great Crested after hearing its loud *"Wheep"* call from the tops of the trees.

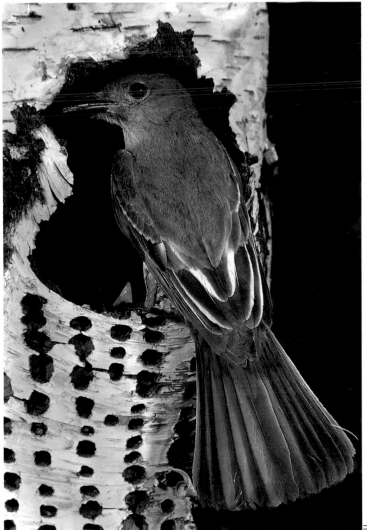

◁ The Great Crested Flycatcher is the only flycatcher in the Northeast which nests in tree cavities and is famous for lining its nestholes with the skins shed by snakes. It also nests in manmade structures such as birdhouses, mailboxes, newspaper tubes, and even the barrels of cannons at historic forts. It fiercely defends its nesting territory against other birds.

◁ Note the pattern of holes which have been drilled in this birch by a Yellowbellied Sapsucker. For more details about sapsuckers, see page 99.

Eastern Kingbird

The kingbird is so named because of its vigorous defense of its nesting territory. Its Latin name, *Tyrannus*, is appropriate to its aggressive nature. It will take on crows and even hawks or owls if they threaten its young.

◁ The Eastern Kingbird has a white band across the end of its square tail. Tail bands are very important field marks. This type is called a terminal band.

◁ This excited Eastern Kingbird is showing its bright head-feathers which are concealed by other feathers and seldom seen unless the bird is alarmed.

Many birds in the genus *Tyrannus* belong to the complex called Tyrant Flycatchers. Only the Eastern Kingbird is *Tyrannus tyrannus*. Usually, double names such as this are given to the species first disovered in that genus (calledthe nominate species).

Frustrating Flycatchers: the Empidonax Complex

Empidonax, "king of the gnats," is the genus name of five of the flycatchers found in the Northeast. This name was probably derived from the fondness of these birds for catching flying insects (although their prey includes beetles, bees and wasps rather than gnats or mosquitos). Four Empidonax flycatchers (the Least, Willow, Alder and Acadian) are very similar in appearance and are almost impossible to identify except by voice. Since they are all silent during migration, they are a constant source of frustration to birders who keep species lists. Many birders just call them "empids."

Least Flycatcher

Eastern Phoebe

The Eastern Phoebe is a small, active flycatcher which says its name *(fee-bee)*. It makes a downward jerking motion with its tail when perched.

△ This photo shows an Eastern Phoebe holding a skipper, a tiny, fast flying butterfly. As can be seen from this photo, Phoebe nests are frequently built under the sheltering eaves of buildings.

△ This wood-pewee is on its "sally perch" from which it will sally forth to capture insects, returning to its perch after each short flight.

Eastern Wood-Pewee

The bristles around the pewee's bill are called rictal bristles and are actually a type of feather, not whiskers or hairs. They help the peewee hunt insects by funneling prey toward its open bill. Note that the pewee's lower bill is yellow, which, along with the pewee's two white wing bars, helps distinguish the pewee from the phoebe.

Gnatcatcher

Blue-gray Gnatcatcher

This small bird does catch gnats (and other insects) for a living. It is often seen in the company of titmice and chickadees. It holds its tail raised at a 45 degree angle much of the time. When chasing insects, the gnatcatcher flits and flutters around like a butterfly and, although drab in color, is fascinating and exciting to observe.

Its call is high-pitched and insect-like. The white ring around its eye is important for identification. It is easily called by making "pishing" sounds, and it frequently comes close to the caller.

In winter, gnatcatchers are often an important part of mixed foraging flocks. Since Blue-gray Gnatcatchers call frequently, birders use them to locate flocks of warblers, since warblers are usually silent during migration.

▽▷The Blue-gray Gnatcatcher builds an elegant nest which resembles that of the Ruby-throated Hummingbird. The nest is held together with spider silk and is covered with lichens on the outside for camouflage.

▷ Notice the worm-eaten leaves in this photo. The presence of insects may have attracted the Blue-gray Gnatcatcher to this particular tree.

The Blue-gray Gnatcatcher, like the cardinal and the titmouse, is extending its range northward, and now nests well into northern New England.

Grackles

Boat-tailed Grackle

In most states Boat-tailed Grackles are found around water, frequently in the same habitats as Red-winged Blackbirds. They especially like cattails and tall weeds around lakes, drainage ditches, standing water, wet meadows, and sometimes open fields. They spend their days foraging for insects and seeds.

Boat-tailed Grackles don't walk so much as strut, always displaying a proud, haughty bearing.

Boat-tailed Grackles are polygynous birds. The males band together in flocks to forage for food, often in the company of Red-winged Blackbirds and Brown-headed Cowbirds. The females visit these flocks and the males may mate with several females. No pair bond is established. The males do not participate in nest building or rearing of the young but may sometimes help defend the nests established by the females.

Boat-tailed Grackles are southern birds who have expanded their range into the Northeast in the past twenty years and are now well established as far north as southern New Jersey. The grackles shown in these photos belong to the southern race and have dark eyes. The Boat-tailed Grackles seen along the Atlantic Coast usually have white or yellow eyes.

Male Boat-tailed Grackle

Female

△ The male-female differences in the Boat-tailed Grackle are very striking. The female is brown, smaller, and hardly looks like the same species.

△ Two Boat-tailed Grackles vocalizing and confronting each other with "bill-tilting" threat displays.

Common Grackle

Notice the striking yellow eyes of the Common Grackle. Crows, Red-winged Blackbirds, Brown-headed Cowbirds, and European Starlings all have dark eyes.

Common Grackles do not demand waterfront living like the Boat-tailed Grackles. They are suburban birds and are frequently seen foraging on lawns. They like populated areas and feed on human debris as well as the food nature provides. When not nesting, grackles tend to roost in remote areas where there are large stands of trees. Flocks of thousands gather together at night in large communal roosts.

Common Grackle

Grosbeaks

Female

Male

Evening Grosbeaks

Evening Grosbeak

The Evening Grosbeak is a frequent visitor to feeding stations in the Northeast (it especially likes sunflower seeds) and is also seen eating the salt used to melt road ice in winter. Note the short tail and prominent white wing patches. There is quite a bit of variation in color among males. The female is more gray than gold, but some people think that the female is more attractive than the gaudy male.

The Evening Grosbeak was at one time thought to sing only in the evening, hence the name, although it is now known that it sings at other times as well.

Evening Grosbeak (male)

Evening Grosbeaks winter erratically in the Northeast from late autumn until spring, when they return to the spruce forests of Canada and northern New England.

Blue Grosbeak

Blue Grosbeak

△ The Blue Grosbeak is a southern bird whose summer range barely extends as far north as southern New York. It winters in Mexico. Note the brownish wing bars which help distinguish this bird from the smaller Indigo Bunting.

Rose-breasted Grosbeak (female)

Rose-breasted Grosbeak (male)

Rose-breasted Grosbeak

The male Rose-breasted Grosbeak sits on a nest to relieve his mate and often sings while sitting on the nest. Rose-breasted Grosbeaks are birds of mature deciduous or mixed forests. They breed in the Northeast in summer, and they winter in Central and South America.

Grouse

Red phase male Ruffed Grouse drumming

Ruffed Grouse

Grouse are like jumbo-sized quail with broad, turkey-like tails. They are sometimes called partridges and are prized by sportsmen as delicious gamebirds. They are also a favorite food of predators such as the fox, bobcat, and lynx.

Grouse are birds of the forest and prosper best in aspen, poplar, and birch habitats. Grouse survive the snows of winter fairly well by eating berries and buds. They do not migrate and spend their lives in small areas.

△▷ The Ruffed Grouse has a red phase and a gray phase, with the color differences occuring mostly in their tails.

Gray phase male Ruffed Grouse

The male Ruffed Grouse finds a "drumming site" such as a fallen log and, while standing upright and braced by his tail, beats his wings to advertise for a mate and to estab-lish territory. At the same time, he will spread the ruff around his neck for dramatic effect. The drumming noise he makes has been compared to the sound of a lawnmower or chainsaw starting up in the dis-tance. The drumming sound car-ries remarkably far.

Red phase male Ruffed Grouse

Spruce Grouse

The Spruce Grouse does eat the needles and buds of spruce trees but also eats those of a number of other trees. It has been heavily hunted as it is an easy target. It was called a Fool Hen by early settlers because they could easily approach and capture it at night as it roosted on low branches.

Hummingbird

Male

Ruby-Throated Hummingbird

The male Ruby-throated Hummingbird has a spectacular patch of red color on its throat. Ornithologists call such throat markings "gorgets." This word formerly referred to a piece of armor which protected the throat and later was used to describe necklaces and throat ornaments worn by stylish ladies.

Female

Iridescent Color in Birds

The jewel-like shimmering color in the feathers of certain birds (such as the throat feathers of the Ruby-throated Hummingbird) is a very special example of nature's beauty. Most ordinary color is produced by pigment. Iridescent color in birds is produced by the structure of certain feathers which act like prisms and break up light into its rainbow hues. That is why the color is not seen in its full brightness unless viewed at the proper angle. In fact, the Ruby-throated Hummingbird's throat looks black when seen from certain angles. If the feathers were plucked from the bird and ground up with a mortar and pestle, the resulting powder would look like mud. The beautiful colors would disappear forever because the prisms would have been destroyed.

Hummingbirds are famous for their ability to hover in the air and for their great speed and agility. They are the only birds capable of flying backwards. Their name comes from the buzzing sound of their wings, which vibrate at up to 70 beats per second. In addition to being the most agile fliers, hummers are also the smallest North American birds. Because of their small size, hummers have a very high rate of metabolism. Their heartbeats range from 500-1000 per minute, and they breathe about 250 times per minute, about 10 times faster than most birds.

Hummingbirds winter in the tropics where they feed on insects. The timing of their migration north depends on the blooming of flowers from which they obtain nectar.

Aztec rulers wore full length garments made of hummingbird skins. In the past century, skins of hummers were shipped to Europe to decorate hats.

Although there are hundreds of species of hummers in the western hemisphere, the Ruby-throated is the only species which breeds in the Northeast. These birds are attracted to the nectar of certain flowers and help pollinate plants in the same manner as insects. They show a distinct preference for red, tubular flowers. Plants which may attract hummers include the trumpet creeper vine, honeysuckle, impatiens, and salvia.

Hummingbirds use their long tongues to gather nectar and to snare small insects. The hollow tongue design allows hummers to sip nectar as if they were using a straw. However, it is a series of short, rapid licks that draws the nectar from the flower. Most feeding is accomplished while hovering, but with certain flowers hummers will alight and take a rest.

Hummers will also sip sugar water from specially designed feeders. In the southwestern states, sugar-water feeders usually attract many hummingbirds.

A Long-Range Bullet

Most hummers migrate south during the winter to Mexico or Central America. Their migration includes a lenghty flight across the Gulf of Mexico.

It is amazing that such tiny birds could store enough fuel for this journey. Yet, they survive over 500 miles of non-stop flight and return in the same manner in the spring. Some Arctic Terns fly across the Atlantic, but they can stop to feed on seafood along the way. There are no flowers available in the Gulf of Mexico to help the hummers. Long ago the mystery of this flight gave rise to wild speculation, including the theory that hummers hitched rides on the backs of larger birds such as hawks. It is possible that hummers make use of favorable winds and it is known that they sometimes land on ships to rest. But the lengthy flight by the tiny birds still remains a great marvel.

△ The hummingbird nest is a tiny cup attached to the limb of a tree. It is usually less than two inches in diameter. It is constructed of soft fibres held together with spider-web material and well camouflaged on the outside with lichens removed from the bark of trees.

The Hummingbird Moth

The Sphinx Moth is sometimes mistaken for a hummingbird because of its high-speed flight, its ability to hover, and its hummingbird-like harvest of nectar from flowers.

Jays

Blue Jay

Blue Jays are members of the crow family and, like crows, are very clever birds. They are also well known for their bold, aggressive manner. Jays sometimes chase pets, plunder eggs from the nests of other birds, and generally dominate the entire backyard. However, jays do benefit other birds in at least one way. They harass owls and hawks and often save small birds at feeders from predation by sounding loud alarm calls. Mockingbirds also give warning calls of danger, but jays are known to sound many false alarms as well. They may do this to clear small birds away from feeders they wish to use, and some experts believe they may even do it just for sport.

Like crows, jays stash excess food in safe places for future use. Nuts and seeds are often hidden. For this reason, Blue Jays are frequently seen dashing around in oak trees. They gather acorns and store many of them just like squirrels. Like squirrels, they often forget where they stored the seeds and thus aid in the distribution of trees to new habitats. In addition to the nuts and seeds, jays will eat just about any food that is available.

The Mechanics of Flight

Birds in flight do not flap their wings directly up and down but bring their wings forward in a rowing motion when beginning each stroke. The tail is used as a brake and a rudder. Note the feathers indicated by the arrow. This is the alula, or "bastard wing." Its function is similar to that of the spoilers which pop up from the wings of jets and other high-performance aircraft during landings. The alula simply directs a stream of air over the wing surface which increases lift and reduces turbulence for improved lift during slow-speed flight. (Look for the alula in the cover photo.)

After the nesting season is finished, baby Blue Jays remain with their family group until they are full grown. They are indistinguishable from the adults by autumn.

This Blue Jay feather is the main (center) tail feather called the middle retrix. Compare it to the feathers in the flight shot (p. 34). Notice that this feather is equal in width on both sides of the its central vane while the others are not. They are all wider on the side closer to the center of the tail. Also, this feather is not very well groomed. This means that it probably did not fall out naturally. It might have been lost in a scuffle with a predator.

Gray Jay

The Gray Jay is a bird of the northern conifer forests. It is smaller than the Blue Jay and has a white crown and black nape. The Gray Jay is tame and often comes to picnic tables looking for scraps of food. Unlike the Blue Jay, the Gray Jay is usually silent.

It usually winters and breeds only as far south as Maine and only rarely moves further south into New England.

Lumbermen in Maine call Gray Jays "gawbies" and try not to harm them as they are thought to bring good luck.

Gray Jay

The Joys of "Anting"

Blue Jays and a number of other birds have been observed flying to ant hills, allowing the ants to climb around on their feathers, and then using their beaks to rub the tiny ants all over their bodies. It is thought that the formic acid from the bodies of the ants works like a natural insecticide to relieve the problems caused by feather mites. Both sunbathing and dust-bathing are believed to serve the same purpose.

Junco

Dark-eyed Junco

The Dark-eyed Junco was formerly called the Slate-colored Junco and the Northern Junco. Notice the dark head and neck with the contrasting white belly and pink beak. The junco has been described as having "dark skies on its back and snow on its belly." It has been called the "gray snowbird." Such a description is especially appropriate, because dark wintry days are the times when this bird is most visible in the Northeast.

Although most juncos pass through the Northeast during their fall migration from Canada to the South, many remain in the Northeast for the winter. These birds are most eager for food handouts from human friends and will readily come to window sills or feeders, although they prefer to feed on the ground. Notice that juncos often flash their tails to expose the white outer feathers when feeding near other birds.

Birders look for the "Oregon" Junco, a race of the Dark-eyed Junco which lives mainly in western North America. Every year a few of these birds are sighted on the East Coast by sharp-eyed amateurs. They resemble the Eastern variety but have reddish-brown wings and backs which contrast strongly with their black heads and necks and their white bellies.

A Bridge Over the Mountains

How do the Oregon Juncos cross the Rocky Mountains to appear on the East Coast? Formerly this mountain range separated the two types of juncos. Only recently was it learned that the two races had linked together and were interbreeding and thus were not different species, as was previously believed. One theory is that increased human population in the Rocky Mountains created a trail of bird feeders which allowed juncos to make their way across the great divide. Another theory is that they were carried across by storms moving west to east.

Killdeer

Broken Wing Display

Killdeer

The Killdeer looks like a sandpiper but is a member of the Plover family. The funny name comes from the sound of this bird's plaintive cry.

Killdeers like open fields and meadows, but a couple of vacant lots in a housing subdivision might be sufficient habitat. They are not, however, backyard birds (unless, of course, your backyard happens to be a large, open meadow).

The Killdeer is best known for its broken-wing act. The Killdeer lays its eggs in open depressions on sandy ground or grassy fields. If an animal or human approaches the eggs, the Killdeer attempts to distract the intruder by dropping a wing, giving a distress call, and fluttering away from the nest. The scientific species name, *vociferus*, is some indication of this bird's ability to attract attention.

There is a fascinating variation to this "distraction display." If the intruder is an animal such as a cow, the Killdeer will fly up into its face until it turns away from the nest. The Killdeer seems to realize that a cow cannot be distracted by a broken wing act in the same manner as a man or a dog.

Why Do Birds Hop?

Some birds hop along the ground while others walk. One reason for this difference is efficiency. Small, short-legged birds can travel farther with a hop than with a step. That is why large, long-legged birds seldom hop.

However, this size theory does not answer the question completely because there are just too many exceptions. For example, Eastern Meadowlarks walk, but the larger Blue Jays hop.

37

Kinglets are tiny, very active birds. In spite of their size, they can withstand cold weather. Most migrate south, but some stay in the northern states throughout the winter.

Golden-crowned Kinglet

Notice that the Golden-crowned has a dark line through its eye rather than the white eye-ring of the Ruby-crowned. The bright patch on the top of its head is not concealed like that of the Ruby-crowned, and the color of the patch indicates the sex of the bird, orange for the male and yellow for the female. The song of the Golden-crowned is so high-pitched that it is above the hearing range of many people.

Golden-crowned Kinglet

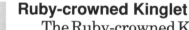

Ruby-crowned Kinglet

The Ruby-crowned Kinglet is a very small bird and it is constantly on the move. Whenever it calls or turns or jumps, it flips its wings almost faster than can be seen. The red crown is seldom noticed, except in the spring when the male may display it to attract a female or to threaten another male. Like the Blue-gray Gnatcatcher, this bird has a white eye-ring. Note that the Ruby-crowned Kinglet's eye-ring is broken; it does not completely encircle the eye.

The Ruby-crowned Kinglet is known for its beautiful songs. For a small bird, it has a very powerful voice.

Ruby-crowned Kinglet

Lark

Horned Lark

The Horned Lark is frequently seen on beaches and dunes as well as salt marshes and fields, and for this reason it is sometimes called the Shore Lark. The Horned Lark is a ground bird and is rarely seen in trees. It runs or walks (but does not hop) and flies up to grasp at tall grasses and shake their seeds to the ground. It also follows cows, looking for undigested grains such as corn, buried in the cow patties.

Notice the two small black horns on its head. These tufts of feathers are not always visible.

Martin

Male in breeding plumage

Purple Martin

Purple Martins are swallows. They arrive in the Northeast in early spring. The male is a dark, shiny blue, but may appear black when the sunlight comes from certain angles. The female is easily distinguished by her light-colored belly and brownish color.

Martins are very popular and people encourage their presence by erecting multi-story bird houses or putting out hollow gourds for nest boxes. Starlings often inhabit the communal nest boxes intended for Purple Martins.

Female Martin

A Clever Way to Sell Bird Houses

Many people believe that Purple Martins eat zillions of mosquitos. This is a myth created by certain manufacturers of those fancy, multi-story martin houses. They have promoted their products as a means to attract Purple Martins and thus biologically control mosquitos. Although Purple Martins do eat mosquitos, most of their diet consists of other insects, including dragonflies. Ironically, the main food of the dragonfly is the mosquito. There are many factors controlling mosquito populations, but martins do not have much effect.

Meadowlark

Eastern Meadowlark

The meadowlark breeds on the ground in thick grasses but is frequently seen sitting on tall grasses, utility poles, or wires, where it is easily visible.

The bright red colors inside the mouths of baby meadowlarks acts as a target and a stimulus for the parent birds to feed the babies.

These colorful mouths are common among the young of those species which are born helpless (altricial birds). Birds that are born self-sufficient (precocial birds), able to feed themselves, lack bright "target" colors.

▷ The meadowlark's call is one of the most pleasant melodies of spring and the meadowlark is one of the earliest migrants to arrive.

A distinctive feature is the black V-shaped marking across the bright yellow breast.

▷ The meadowlark nest resembles a tunnel of grass.

Fecal Sacs

Amazingly, the waste material (bird droppings) excreted by bird nestlings comes wrapped in thin, watertight membranes. These little packages are easily removed from the nest by the parent birds. Some parents actually swallow the fecal sacs since the baby birds do not do a very good job of digestion and there is still quite a bit of food value left in them.

▷ Note the beautiful pattern of the meadowlark's back and the white patch on each side of its tail. If it turns its head, this meadowlark will disappear.

Despite its bright color, the Eastern Meadowlark is a member of the blackbird family. This classification is based upon internal anatomy as well as external features such as bill, legs and feet, and wings and tail.

Mockingbird

Northern Mockingbird

The scientific name, *Mimus polyglottos,* means "mimic of many tongues," a good description of the mockingbird. The "mocker" is a superb songster with many beautiful melodies of its own as well as the ability to imitate the songs of other birds and any man-made noises that come to its attention.

> ### A World-Class Performer
> *Many experts consider the mockingbird to be the finest songbird in the world in terms of its huge repertoire and the number of performances given. There is a theory that birds that are ordinary in color are more gifted in song. The mockingbird is often cited as an example.*

Property Rights

Mockingbirds are very territorial. They establish and defend a breeding territory around their nests in the spring and a food-gathering territory in the fall. Their prolific songs help to mark and establish these territories.

"Haves" Versus the "Have-Nots"

The "landed-gentry," those mockingbirds with established territories, seem capable of recognizing a common interest. They will sometimes set aside their bickering and band together for a few moments to help a neighboring mocker repel an intruder who has no territory of its own!

Mockers are famous for attacking intruders to their nesting territories. Their targets include cats, dogs, squirrels, and people, as well as other birds. Their diving attacks have reduced many a household pet to a nervous wreck when the poor animal merely ventured into its own backyard.

◁ Mockers are so territorial that they do not hesitate to attack their own images in mirrors or windows. The mocker believes that the reflected image is another bird invading its territory.

△ Mockers benefit other small birds by harassing large birds. Here a mocker chases a crow.

△ The beautiful eggs of the mockingbird are a delicate blue color perfectly complemented by soft brown spots.

They Sing at Night

A few birds can be heard singing after dark. The mockingbird may sit in one tree and continue his music all night long. Studies have shown that only unmated males sing at night, although it is not known for sure that the purpose of the song is to attract a mate.

Other night singers include the Bobwhite, Common Nighthawk, Chuck-wills-widow, Whip-poor-will, Killdeer, and White-throated Sparrow.

Wing Flashing

The mockingbird sits on a perch and observes a yard or open field. When opportunity knocks, the mocker will fly down from its perch and dash about on the ground, frequently spreading its wings. There is a large white patch on each wing, and it is thought that by flashing these bright spots, the mockingbird frightens insects, causing them to jump and reveal their locations. Some researchers have suggested other functions for wingflashing such as territorial defense. The true nature of this behavior is still debated.

The fuzz on the top of this baby mocker's head is not hair but the last residue of baby down feathers. Down feathers disappear from the head last.

The Case of the Bigamous Mocker

Bigamy is unusual with mockingbirds but, as with humans, it is not unknown. A university researcher followed the marital stress endured by one sexually ambitious mockingbird during an entire breeding season. This bird had established two nests with different mates, but feeding the young of both was too much burden for one bird to bear. He chose to feed the young of one female for a while and then abruptly switched to the other rather than trying to support both at the same time. The resulting hardship to the young birds who were only fed by their mothers caused some loss of nestlings. However, researchers noted that this male was more aggressive than average. His success in defending both nests against intruders may have made up for his inability to feed both sets of young. Why did the second female choose a male who was already mated (although unmated males were available)? Her decision may have been influenced by the male's unusual aggressiveness. Her choice of such a mate may have actually increased the chances for survival of her chicks.

The "Border Dance"

Two mockers will meet eye to eye along the boundary line between their territories. They jump from side to side, each following the other's movements, reaffirming the boundaries, and then, usually, each will fly back into its own territory without a fight.

Nightjars

Whip-poor-will

There are three types of Nightjars in the Northeast, and they all look remarkably similar, except for some small size differences.

Whip-poor-will

The call of the Whip-poor-will is perfectly described by its name. It can be so persistent throughout the night as to drive one to drink. The Whip-poor-will is only found in certain localized areas of the Northeast, but its call makes its presence well known in those places.

The Whip-poor-will is a member of a group of birds known as nightjars or goat-suckers. The name "nightjar" refers to their tendency to disturb the night with their calls.

The name "goat-sucker" derives from an ancient belief that these birds milked the udders of goats for nourishment and that the goats sometimes went blind as a consequence.

Chuck-wills-widow

The *"WHIP-poor-WILL"* sound is a very common night-time cry in rural areas, but the cry of the Chuck-wills-widow is very similar. If you are close enough you will hear that each verse is preceded by a soft "chuck" sound. This is primarily a southern bird whose range extends northward only to southern New Jersey.

◁⇕ The Chuck-wills-widow is larger and more brownish than the very similar Whip-poor-will. Note the whiskers which help funnel insects into the large mouth during flight.

44

Common Nighthawk

Nighthawks can sometimes be spotted on a tree branch, in ground-cover, or on a stump or fence. In spite of their superb camouflage and their ability to sit motionless, a lucky birder walking through the area will occasionally get a glimpse of one.

Nighthawks eat mostly insects, especially moths, and are well equipped for the job with huge, scoop-like mouths. Surrounding their mouths are long whiskers which help funnel insect prey into the mouth opening.

It is believed that some nightjars have a sonar system, like bats, which helps to locate prey in the dark and also helps avoid collisions with trees during night flights.

The Common Nighthawk hunts insects on the wing, and it is easily recognized by the white marking under

Common Nighthawk

each wing. It is the only nightjar that is active at sunset time or earlier. If you are driving along a country road at dusk or at night and see a rapidly moving bird with a white mark on each wing criss-crossing the road, it is most likely a nighthawk. They often hunt over roads. In some parts of the country, this bird is called a "bullbat" because of its bat-like feeding behavior.

Nighthawks are not hawks despite their name. Among other important differences, they lack the strong talons that are common to the birds of prey. Since nighthawks hunt insects by scooping them up in their mouths, they have no need for strong claws.

Nighthawks often nest on the roofs of buildings. Another Northeast bird found nesting on roofs is the Killdeer.

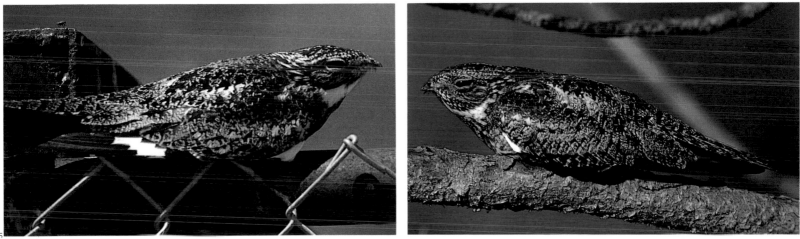

△ These nighthawks are perched in a "protective crouch" which helps them to blend with a branch or fence for better camouflage.

▽ In flight the Common Nighthawk shows a white bar on each wing which is very handy for identification.

Nuthatches

White-breasted Nuthatch

The nuthatch has been called the upside-down bird. It is famous as the only bird which travels headfirst down tree trunks while foraging for insects. This habit gives it the advantage of discovering food missed by other species that may have inspected the same tree but only in an upward direction. The nuthatch manages its acrobatic act by spreading its legs to the front and back. It hangs from the toes of the rear foot while using its front foot for balance.

Europeans called this bird the "nuthack" after watching it put soft-shelled seeds, such as acorns and chestnuts, in crevices and forks of tree branches and hack them open with its beak. The name evolved to nuthatch in this country, as the bird "hatches" the kernel from its shell. Notice the black cap, the white underparts including the face, and the short squarish tail. The slightly upturned, chisel-like beak is another trademark.

White-breasted Nuthatch

Red-breasted Nuthatch

Red-breasted Nuthatch

In addition to its reddish breast color, this nuthatch features a black line through its eye and a white line above the eye.

The Red-breasted Nuthatch may appear in large numbers in the Northeast in winter if the annual seed crop in Canada, on which it depends for food, is poor.

Although both nuthatches nest in tree cavities, the Red-breasted has the habit of smearing pine pitch around its nest entrance to discourage predators such as snakes and also other birds competing for the same nest site.

Northern Oriole

This bird used to be known as the Baltimore Oriole, but ornithologists decided that it should be included in the same species as a very similar western bird formerly called Bullock's Oriole. Now both birds have been grouped together and are simply called Northern Orioles.

Orioles are famous for their carefully constructed, hanging nests, usually situated near the outer branches of an elm, maple or linden tree. The nests are well made and seldom blow down, even in heavy storms.

If an oriole starts building a nest in your yard, try putting out pieces of brightly colored yarn. The oriole will likely weave them into its nest. Orioles can often be attracted to a feeder by hanging up a section of an orange.

Orchard Oriole

The Orchard Oriole is smaller than the Northern Oriole. It is also darker and more reddish-brown. It is more of a southern bird and less common in the Northeast.

It can also build a woven nest, but the nest of the Orchard Oriole does not hang. It usually rests in the fork of a tree's branches.

Orchard Oriole

Pheasant

Ring-necked Pheasant

The Ring-necked Pheasant is native to Asia but was introduced to Europe, originally as an ornamental bird. Later, after the development of firearms, including the shotgun, it became very popular with European huntsmen as a gamebird. It was introduced to North America about 100 years ago.

The Ring-necked Pheasant often has a hard time obtaining food in the winter when the ground is covered with snow and it even resorts to scavenging for garbage in populated areas. It is dependent to some extent on the grain put out in winter by sportsmen interested in maintaining pheasant populations for hunting. It attempts to survive in woodland environments and marshes, but it is especially attracted to the grain from agricultural fields.

Pheasant cocks fight over females in the spring, and the early morning hours in some areas are filled with the sound of their crowing as loud challenges are made and answered. Males that are victorious in the ensuing battles accumulate harems of many hens as the reward for their effort.

Hen pheasant after ice storm

Ptarmigan

Willow Ptarmigan

Willow Ptarmigan are Arctic grouse which are sometimes found as far south as Maine but seldom, if ever, seen farther south. They are popular as gamebirds and striking in their appearance in winter when their brown plumage changes to snowy white!

Ptarmigan stay on the ground in the face of danger long enough for a hunter to approach within shotgun range and then explode into the air with incredible acceleration, providing a challenging target.

This bird is known as the "Willow" Ptarmigan because in winter it eats the buds and twigs of the willow tree (and those of the alder, birch, and other trees as well). "Ptarmigan" is pronounced *"tar-mi-gen."*

Note the scarlet wattle over the eye of the male in summer breeding plumage. Birders sometimes call this feature "red eyebrows."

The feathered feet of the Willow Ptarmigan may be of help in walking on snow. The feathers reach all the way to the tips of the toes and may also protect against cold.

Winter

Male in Summer

Bird Names

The American Ornithologists Union determines the common and scientific names of birds and periodically renames birds to align their names with the names of other species around the world. It also renames birds when species are combined. Birders usually prefer scientific names because common names change more often and can be confusing.

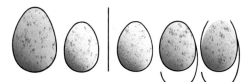

Oology: Even the Word Itself Looks Like a Box of Eggs!

Oology is the study of bird eggs. It was a very popular hobby in the previous century but impossible now, because of the laws protecting wild birds and their nests. However, surviving egg collections and notes taken by the collectors have helped present-day ornithologists in a number of ways. For example, to determine whether a species has declined in numbers, ornithologists may seek records kept by oologists a hundred years ago to get some indication of the number of bird nests in certain areas.

Another valuable use of these collections is to determine the thickness of eggshells prior to the use of DDT. Although egg collecting is illegal in England, there are still more than 600 known "eggers" in that country who flout the law and risk prosecution to pursue their hobby. Penalties can include confiscation of their collections and their vehicles, plus jail. One egger whose truck had been confiscated was recently interviewed after being released from jail. While the interview was being conducted, he was diligently at work constructing a wooden cabinet with dozens of drawers only a few inches deep, and each drawer divided into hundreds of small, egg-sized compartments. When asked the purpose of the cabinet, he replied that he was going to use it to "store his pants."

Redpoll

Common Redpoll

Redpolls nest in the far north of Canada and are only found in the northeastern United States in winter. They can be very abundant in certain years. They eat the seeds of birches and alders, and weeds, and commonly visit feeders. The red cap and black markings under its chin distinguishes this bird from the similar-sized Pine Siskin.

Common or Uncommon?

Crossbills and redpolls are birds that tend to be nomadic. Some winters they may appear in large numbers in the Northeast. In other winters they may not be seen at all. Their nomadic nature is related to fluctuations in their food supply. When the supply of birch seeds is good, redpolls remain in the Arctic and Subarctic. Likewise, a good crop of pine seeds will keep the crossbills at home. Should the crop of birch or pine seeds be poor in a given year, then these birds head south in search of food.

51

Robin

American Robin

Robins are among the best known and most loved of American birds. They arrive early in spring, stay late into the fall, have a cheery song, and are most attractive with their red and black colors. They were named by the early settlers who compared them to the English Robins, birds which also have red breasts but are much smaller. The English Robin, like its American cousin, is a member of the thrush family.

△ This robin is collecting insects for its young and is about to fly back to its nest. Feeding for itself only, a robin would swallow the insects as soon as they were caught.

▽ This flock of robins in the snow consists of bachelor males which have arrived in the north a few weeks ahead of the females during spring migration.

△ This Robin's nest has been parasitized by a cowbird. The cowbird eggs are the spotted eggs. The Robin's eggs are a special greenish-blue color which has been popularized by interior decorators as "robin's-egg blue."

Female with worms

Going for the Whole Worm

Robins exert slow, steady pressure when pulling worms from the ground in order to avoid breaking them in half. Robins find worms visually. They often tilt their heads to one side while hunting. A robin's eyes are positioned far back on the side of its head and it is easier to focus on a close object with one eye only. Many species of worms rest with the tips of their bodies protruding slightly from their tunnels. It is these worm tips that the robin spots.

Robins on a Lawn

The seemingly random motions of robins zig-zagging across a lawn are due to the fact that a robin's eyes cannot be moved much in their sockets. Rather than turn its head while feeding, the robin turns its body to look for new opportunities. At the same time, each robin tries to avoid facing directly to- ward another member of its flock, red breast to red breast, a stance which might trigger aggression. Robins feed together in a flock in the early morning hours, but by afternoon, most robins are feeding alone. The reason for this difference in morning and afternoon behavior is not known.

Shrikes

Loggerhead Shrike

The shrike is famous for its habit of storing food on the sharp points of broken twigs, barbed wire, or thorny vegetation. Thus, it has earned the nickname "butcher bird." In northern states, the sharp thorn of a tree or bush is most commonly used (hawthorne is a favorite). Shrikes are among the very few North American songbirds that are regular predators of small mammals and birds as well as insects.

The shrike has a sharply hooked beak which helps capture live prey, and a close view reveals black whiskers. From a distance, a shrike could be confused with a mockingbird, but shrikes have heavy black masks over their eyes and a more compact shape.

The flight of the shrike is distinctive. When flying from perch to perch, the shrike will suddenly drop to nearly ground level, fly the distance close to the ground, and then ascend sharply to the new perch.

The Loggerhead Shrike is a southern bird that is not common in the Northeast. Its numbers have been declining throughout the eastern part of its range in recent years.

The shrike relies heavily on barbed wire fences and the thorns of plants for its meat rack. If you notice an insect impaled on the points of a barbed wire fence, there is very likely a shrike working the surrounding territory.

Songs -vs- Call Notes

△ The name "shrike" probably comes from the word "shriek," because of this bird's harsh call note, but its song is melodic and quite pleasant. "Call notes" are different from songs. Songs are complex melodies usually heard during the breeding season when birds are marking territories and attracting mates. Call notes are brief sounds of one or two syllables which are used year round. They have many purposes including alarm, uniting family members, and summoning help.

Northern Shrike

The Northern Shrike is a Canadian bird that winters sporadically in New England. Any shrike seen in the Northeast in winter is almost certainly this species.

The Northern Shrike is slightly larger than the Loggerhead, and its black face mask does not extend across the top of its bill as does the mask of the Loggerhead. Also, its lower bill is not solid black like that of the Loggerhead.

Siskin

Pine Siskin

The Pine Siskin is a small finch which lives in forests of cone-bearing trees. During migration it is frequently seen in flocks with other species, such as the goldfinch, feeding on the seeds of weeds and grasses. It often comes to feeders in the winter and, like the goldfinch, is particularly fond of thistle seed.

Note the heavy streaking of the Pine Siskin and the notched tail. Look for a touch of yellow in both the wings and the tail.

Siskins are closely related to goldfinches and red-polls, and the winter flocking habits of these species are quite similar as are their constant chattering calls.

Siskins are fond of eating road salt and because of this habit, many siskins are killed by cars.

Snipe

Common Snipe

Many people think there is no such thing as a snipe because of a traditional prank played on children arriving at summer camp for the first time. The newcomers are given a bag and sent out into the darkness with instructions to "catch a snipe." They return exhausted and empty-handed hours later to the jeers of the older campers.

Snipes really do exist, but they are hard to find, even by experienced birders searching in broad daylight.

The snipe has a territorial display in which it dives through the air with its tail feathers spread apart, creating a loud whistling noise.

The name "snipe" may be derived from the Dutch word "snippen," meaning "to snap," a reference to the sound of a beak closing sharply.

△ Snipe usually live around ponds and other wet areas where they probe the ground with their long beaks searching for worms and grubs. The tip of the snipe's beak is soft and full of nerve endings which allow the snipe to smell and feel the movements and scents of various types of prey. When flushed, snipe give their harsh call, "Snipe", and fly off in a zig-zag pattern.

◁ The fanned tail of the male snipe is part of its courtship display as it pursues a female who is a potential mate.

Sparrows

House Sparrow

The bird most people think of as a sparrow is not really a sparrow at all but a member of the Weaver Finch family. This is the House Sparrow, sometimes called the English Sparrow. It was introduced from Europe in the 1850's and, like the starling, has become one of the most common birds in the United States.

House Sparrows are especially common around man. One might think that they live primarily around city parks and exist on a diet of leftover potato chips and french fries. This is not far from the truth. These little birds make good use of man-made environments for both food and shelter.

In the wilds of Africa, some species of weaver finches produce woven nests. But in this country, the House Sparrow confines itself to nesting near man, often using man-made structures for nest sites and human trash for food. Sometimes large shaggy nests are found in trees, but they are not well made like those of the House Sparrow's African kin.

Male

Male (left) with female

All-Electric Home

House Sparrows frequently nest inside lighted outdoor signs. These nests must be nice and warm in winter. Any small opening which allows access to a building or man-made structure will invite a sparrow family to set up house-keeping.

Swamp Sparrow

△▷ This dark-colored sparrow lives in the swampy areas around rivers, lakes and wet meadows.

Flights of Caution

House Sparrows and a number of other small birds interrupt their feeding at frequent intervals to fly off to a perch and then quickly return. This repeated motion follows a rhythmic pattern and is a precaution against unseen predators.

Sparrows

Chipping Sparrow

Chipping Sparrows often live in gardens and will come to feeders. They are common at picnic tables and are very tame. The Chipping Sparrow is seen in the summer in the Northeast.

△ Note the white eyebrow and black line through the eye. Chipping Sparrows are named for the rapid, staccato notes of their songs.

Savannah Sparrow

▽ Note the yellow eyebrow and notched tail. This sparrow likes wide open spaces such as fields, salt marshes, and coastal dunes. Seventeen races of the Savannah Sparrow have been identified.

Field Sparrow

△ The Field Sparrow is found in meadows which have become overgrown with bushes. The pinkish bill makes this bird easy to recognize. Note also the white eye-ring and reddish cap.

White-throated Sparrow

The White-throated Sparrow sings some of the most beautiful songs of any bird. Banding studies have shown that migrating White-throated Sparrows tend to return to the same place every year, sometimes even the same tree or bush. Note the black and white stripes on the head which, along with the white throat and yellow lores (bare skin around the eyes), make identification easy.

Grasshopper Sparrow

◁ This small, brown-streaked bird is an inhabitant of grassy fields. It is secretive in its habits and easier to hear than to see. It derives its name from the thin, insect-like buzz that constitutes its song. Both males and females sing. During the nesting season, the song of the Grasshopper Sparrow can often be heard at night.

Song Sparrow

▷ In the Northeast the Song Sparrow is often seen in wooded suburbs along with the Chipping Sparrow. Note the heavy streaking and dark spot on the breast. In flight, the Song Sparrow is known for the pumping motion of its tail.

There is a wide dispersal of this species from Alaska to Newfoundland and south throughout the US to Mexico. It varies in size, color, and even song by subtle differences, yet in every case, the bird is easily identified.

Dusting

Dust bathing is thought to offer some relief from feather mites. Small craters are dug into sand and the birds flutter their wings and go through bathing motions, allowing the warm sand to flow over their feathers. It may be the heat of the sand which is the attraction as birds are also known to puff their feathers out and sunbathe (see pigeon photo, page 17). Sparrows are the birds which are most frequently seen dusting. Once a good site is located, they tend to return repeatedly to the same hollows in the sand.

Fox Sparrow

The Fox Sparrow is one of the largest sparrows. It has a clear, flute-like song and lives in dense woodland thickets where it rummages through leaves on the ground. Its name refers to its reddish tail and reddish markings which bring to mind the coloration of the Red Fox.

White-crowned Sparrow

The White-crown is a regular but scarce fall migrant in the Northeast. It is even rarer in the spring, being present for only brief stops as it rushes to its breeding grounds in eastern Canada. Its pink bill is a handy field mark for distinguishing this sparrow from its close relative, the White-throated Sparrow.

His Eye is on the Sparrow

Although the sparrow is often overlooked because it is so small and common, it has received an unusual amount of attention in literature and the Bible. Shakespeare's Hamlet proclaimed, "There is a special providence in the fall of a sparrow," a reference to the passages in the book of Matthew in which Jesus used this seemingly insignificant little bird to make a point about how God provides for all his creatures. "Look at the birds of the air; they neither sow nor reap nor gather into barns, and yet your heavenly Father feeds them. Are you not of more value than they?" (Matthew 6: 26.) "Are not two sparrows sold for a penny? And not one of them will fall to the ground without your Father's will. Fear not, therefore; you are of more value than many sparrows." (Matthew 10: 29-31)

American Tree Sparrow

▷ This sparrow migrates south from its northern breeding grounds to winter in the northern states and southern Canada. It is often seen at feeders. Note the chestnut-colored crown and the beak which is dark above and yellow below.

Seaside Sparrow

▽ The Seaside Sparrow is a resident of salt marshes along the coast as far north as Massachusetts. This restricted habitat has led to reduced populations as coastal areas continue to be developed and salt marshes disappear. There are several races, or subspecies, of Seaside Sparrows.

Vesper Sparrow

The Vesper Sparrow is so named because it frequently sings in the early evening, but it also sings during the day. Note the eye-ring and the reddish patch on its wing.

Sharp-tailed Sparrow

This bird is found in coastal salt marshes. It prefers to run along the ground, and when flushed, remains low in flight until cover can be reached. Its tail is not actually pointed, or sharp, but the individual feathers of the tail each come to a sharp point.

The Sharp-tailed Sparrow is called the "mouse-bird" of coastal marshes. It prefers to hide in the grasses until flushed. It will fly a short distance, drop to the ground, and then run through the grass like a small brown mouse.

61

Starling

European Starling

The starling is one of the most common birds in the Northeast and may be the most common bird in the United States. In 1890, a small flock of starlings was released in New York City. They were a part of one man's strange idea to bring to America all the birds mentioned in Shakespeare's plays.* Since then, the starling has proved itself to be one of the most adaptable and resilient bird species.

By prospering to such a degree, the starling has made a pest of itself in many ways. Starlings have taken over nesting holes needed to maintain the population of bluebirds, Tree Swallows, and other birds that nest in cavities. They also take over woodpecker nest holes, but woodpeckers are capable of carving new nests for themselves. Starlings are more of a threat to birds that must find nest holes and cannot construct their own.

Starlings love airports and have caused airplane crashes by clogging jet engines with their bodies. In the winter, they travel in huge flocks along with blackbirds and cause problems wherever they decide to roost. Entire woods are made white with their droppings. Tree branches are broken from the weight of so many roosting birds.

Summer

Winter

The starling in summer is black with iridescent blue and green colors. Note the coral-colored legs and bright yellow bill.

In winter its plumage becomes brightly speckled, and the bird looks strikingly different. The yellow bill seen in summer becomes dark for the winter.

This Isn't Snow!

△ After the starlings and blackbirds leave, the branches are covered with their droppings.

First Part of Henry IV, Act I, Scene III, Line 224: "But... I will find him when he lies asleep, and in his ear I'll hollow 'Mortimer.' Nay, I'll have a starling shall be taught to speak nothing but 'Mortimer,' and give it to him to keep his anger still in motion."

◁ A roosting flock of starlings covers a bare tree like leaves. Often such flocks include large numbers of Red-winged Blackbirds. In some places starlings have become a nuisance because of their large roosting flocks. Efforts to exterminate them include spraying them with soapy water on very cold nights. The soap removes oil from their feathers, the feathers absorb water, and the birds freeze to death.

Swallows

Tree Swallow

Swallows are very similar to swifts, except that they are capable of perching. They migrate in large flocks and on their wintering grounds may devour wild berries in large quantities. NASA had to remove the wax myrtles at the edge of the Space Shuttle landing strip because they were attracting thousands of Tree Swallows. After gorging themselves, they would then sunbathe on the runway, creating a hazard.

In the Northeast, the bulk of the Tree Swallow's diet consists of insects which they catch on the wing. They will eat berries in the Northeast, but only when forced to do so.

> ### The Bluebird Connection
> *Tree Swallows nest in holes in trees (hence their name), but readily accept man-made nest boxes. Bluebird lovers often build pairs of nest boxes back-to-back. Tree Swallows will not allow other birds of their own species to nest close by, so if Tree Swallows move into one of the boxes, they will defend the other box against any other Tree Swallows, and at least one of the nest boxes in the pair will remain available for bluebirds. Once both are settled, Tree Swallows have no objection to bluebirds as neighbors.*

Tree Swallows form large flocks during fall migration. Tree Sparrows resemble female Purple Martins but have whiter breasts. The Tree Swallow's species name, *bicolor*, reflects its white breast's contrast to its dark back.

Cliff Swallow

This swallow builds globe-shaped nest of mud under the eaves of buildings or on the sides of dirt cliffs or banks. Note the white forehead.

Collecting mud for nest

Bank Swallow

Bank Swallows build nests in large colonies on the vertical surfaces of river banks, mining pits, and road cuts. Their Latin name, *Riparia,* means the bank of a river. Notice the solid brown band across the chest.

Barn Swallow

Barn Swallow

The Barn Swallow is the only swallow in the Northeast that has a truly forked "swallow tail." The Barn Swallow is also easy to distinguish because of its rust-colored under-parts. It builds its mud nest under the roofs of buildings, especially barns.

Swallows do their feeding away from their nests. For this reason, they defend a rather small nesting territory.

Rough-winged Swallow

The Rough-winged Swallow does have some unusual primary feathers, hence its name. It looks like the Bank Swallow, but is larger, lacks the breast band, and does not nest in colonies.

Barn Swallow nest

Rough-winged Swallow

Every Barn Should Have Them

According to folklore, a barn which has Barn Swallows nesting within, will not be struck by lightning. Statistics to prove or disprove this notion are not readily available.

Do the Famous Mission Swallows Really Return on the Same Day?

There is a legend that a flock of Cliff Swallows in California returns to the Mission of El Capistrano on exactly the same day every year. Newspapers nationwide cover the event. The birds do return with regularity, but the idea that they return on the same day is a myth. The date may vary as much as a week or so either way.

Swift

Chimney Swift

The Chimney Swift catches insects in flight. It spends most of its time in the air and can even mate without landing, although mating also occurs at the nest. Swifts are indeed very swift. Some species can fly over 100 miles per hour, although the swifts in the Northeast are not that fast. They generally do not fly at top speed because they must make quick turns while hunting their insect prey.

The Chimney Swift creates its nest with small twigs held together with saliva that is especially sticky. The swift's huge saliva glands undergo an enormous enlargement during the breeding season. The nests are usually built in hollow trees, corners of buildings and as their name implies, inside unused chimneys.

MH/Cornell

The Chimney Swift has sharp claws which are adapted for clinging to a vertical surface and are not very useful for walking. Since perching is not necessary, all four toes are pointed forward for extra clinging ability. The short, stiff, square tail of the Chimney Swift is used as an extra support by the bird when it clings to walls.

A Rare and Expensive Gourmet Food

Some Asian species of swifts create their nests in large caves and build them almost entirely of saliva. These nests are the source of a Chinese delicacy, bird's nest soup. This mild tasting concoction is very expensive. The nests are built very high in rocky caves and can only be gathered by using tall ladders. It is a very difficult and dangerous job. Bird's nest soup is valued for its medicinal properties. It is thought to be a health-giving tonic.

The Prison with No Doors

How does a baby bird escape from its eggshell? Most baby birds are equipped with an "egg tooth," a projection on the tip of the beak which helps weaken the egg. The egg tooth strikes the shell as a result of a series of surges by a special muscle on the back of the head and neck called the hatching muscle. After the first tiny break in the shell, the hatchling twists around inside the shell and repeats the process in a different area until the shell has been cut open.

How Birds Are Counted

Bird counts by professionals or skilled amateurs measure bird populations. But how do you avoid double counting when birds can fly around as the count progresses? Its easy during the breeding season, when birds form territories and tend to stay in them, but at other times of the year, counting migrating or foraging flocks can be difficult at best. Double counting is always a danger, and the people involved in these counts use care and do the best they can.

Tanagers

Scarlet Tanager

The beautiful Scarlet Tanager breeds in the Northeast in summer. It winters in South America and the name, tanager, comes from a South American Indian word. The red body with black wings is a unique pattern among North American birds.

Molting Summer Tanager

The New Wardrobe

Molting is the process by which birds replace old feathers. Some species molt in spring, just before the breeding season when a bird needs brilliant new feathers to attract a mate. Virtually all species molt at the close of the breeding season. The brilliant colors are no longer needed and might attract predators. Birds loose their feathers gradually, so they are never really naked, although some waterbirds become flightless for a week or so. The photo above shows the intermediate stage of the Scarlet Tanager's molt. It is called "eclipse plumage" because the colors become dim like the sun during an eclipse. Later, all the red will disappear.

Summer Tanager

The Summer Tanager is basically a southern species that nests as far north as Pennsylvania and New Jersey. Elsewhere in the Northeast it is seen as a rare spring or fall migrant. It spends the winter months in Central and South America.

The Summer Tanager is sometimes mistaken for a cardinal but has no crest. It eats insects which it catches in flight or by gleening from the leaves and branches of trees.

Male Scarlet Tanager

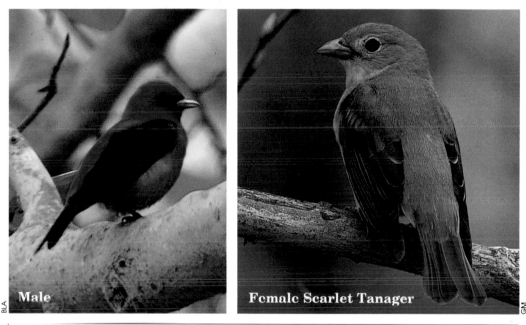

Male

Female Scarlet Tanager

The Duller Sex

Why are female birds usually much duller in color than males? Nature has gifted them with much better protective coloration. This camouflage helps them survive when they are confined to the nest during the breeding season. The brightly colored males are more obvious targets for predators.

Male Summer Tanager

Thrasher

Brown Thrasher

The Brown Thrasher is commonly seen foraging in piles of leaves or at the edges of tall grass or scrub plants. It is sometimes mistaken for a thrush, but it has a slender body and longer tail and its underparts are streaked rather than spotted. It has a distinctively longer bill and a beautiful, bright yellow eye.

The Brown Thrasher is closely related to the mockingbird, and except for its color, the resemblance is clear. Note the long tail, the beak, and its general size and shape. Also, like the mockingbird, the Brown Thrasher is a skilled singer.

The Meaning of "Rufous"

If you are not yet a birder, you may think "rufous" is a character in the Gasoline Alley comic strip. Actually, the fellow's name is spelled "Rufus." But "rufous" refers to a certain reddish-brown color. The word is sometimes used by artists and, for some reason, is used with great frequency in describing birds. The back of the Brown Thrasher is a good example of this special color.

Keeping Score at Your Feeder

By observing and recording which birds are chased away from your feeder and by which species, you can determine a general pecking order for your backyard. Not every feeder will be the same, and the pecking order may change with the seasons. Also, hunger may make an individual bird unusually aggressive and completely upset the normal pecking order.

Thrushes

Wood Thrush

These birds are smaller than the rather similar Brown Thrasher. Also, their breasts are spotted rather than streaked, and they are chunkier birds.

Many thrush nests are found in the Christmas trees that are shipped to market for holiday decorations.

While the various species of thrushes in the Northeast may look alike, their songs are very different.

I Wish I May, I Wish I Mite

If every little birdie had its wish, the pesky feather mites that infest all birds would disappear. Mites are arachnids, tiny creatures related to spiders. They live on birds and eat their feathers and flakes of their skin. Birds have other parasites such as feather lice which do much the same thing. Dust baths, sunbathing, and anting are ways in which birds try to alleviate the itching caused by mites. Mites help scientists establish species of birds because a species of mite living on one species of bird is never found on a different bird species.

Thrushes

Hermit Thrush

The Hermit is the last to leave the Northeast in the fall. Any thrush seen after October is almost certainly a Hermit.

Veery

The Veery is known for its clear song often heard at twilight time. It says part of its name, "veer." The Veery can be swift in migration. A Veery banded in Canada was recaptured two days later in Florida.

Veery

BD/Cornell

What does "Species" mean?

The definition of "species" has changed through the years, and it is still difficult at times for ornithologists to decide how to classify a certain bird. That is why bird names are sometimes changed as new information appears. It is also why birds within a species are sometimes further divided into "subspecies" (also called "races").

At first, ornithologists depended upon similarities in appearance. The next standard was whether the birds could breed in the wild and produce viable offspring. At one time, even song patterns were considered in classification. The latest approach involves the study of similarities in DNA structure.

Bird watchers are sometimes annoyed when species are changed, because if two species are combined, it may reduce the number of birds on their lists. But advances in scientific knowledge require that classifications be updated once in a while. A committee of the American Ornithologists Union (AOU) is the final arbiter of these questions.

Hermit Thrush (Note the reddish tail)

Veery

Swainson's Thrush

Note the buff-colored eye-ring which distinguishes this bird from other thrushes.

Swainson's Thrush

Titmouse

Tufted Titmouse

The titmouse is considered a leader of the "mixed flocks" of small birds that gather in the winter. Its song sounds like *"peter, peter, peter."*

It is a close relative of the Chickadee. In recent years the Titmouse has been extending its range northward, perhaps because it is a feeder bird and there are a lot more people operating bird feeders today.

The prominent crest on the head of the titmouse is used in aggresive displays.

The Fine Art of Pishing

It may sound a little vulgar, but "pishing" is what birders call the "Pshhhhh, pshhhhh, pshhhhh" sound they make to attract those little birds (such as titmice) which ordinarily stay hidden. This noise sounds like another bird scolding a predator, such as an owl. The small birds all quickly come to investigate. If a real owl was discovered, a group of small birds would gang up to harass him and chase him away. Playing a tape-recorded owl call will also work, but "pishing" is much more convenient and less stressful to the birds.

A Good Reason to Lay Eggs

Imagine how difficult flight would be if a female bird had to undergo pregnancy in the same manner as mammals. Bats are mammals that fly and still manage to give birth to live young, so it is not impossible. Yet, the ability to reproduce by laying eggs gives birds an advantage which may have improved their ability to fly and thus helped them to prosper.

Towhee

Male

Rufous-Sided Towhee

The towhee says its name. In some places it is also called the "chewink," a name which sounds like another one of the towhee's calls. Some people think the call sounds like *"jo-ree,"* and so it earns yet another name.

The towhee has interesting feeding habits. It forages along the ground in brush piles, leaves, and heavy undergrowth. It kicks backwards with both feet at the same time to rake away leaves and expose seeds and insects on the ground. This motion has been described as "hopping in place." The towhee is one of only a few birds in the world to use this double-kicking method of foraging.

Towhees are not common in backyards, but when they do appear at feeding trays, they use the same kicking motion even though the seeds are in plain view. The result is that the food on the tray is scattered.

In Florida, a resident race of towhees has light-colored eyes. The towhees in other parts of eastern North America have red eyes. The red-eyed birds and the white-eyed birds used to be considered separate species, but now they are grouped together because they can interbreed. Some southern towhees have orange eyes.

Female

The female Rufous-sided Towhee is similar to the male, but in the parts where the male is black, the female is brown and it is duller overall.

Notice the yellow eyes of this towhee. It is an example of the southern race. Also note the leafy habitat where the towhee forages.

Turkey

Wild Turkey

The Spanish explorers were very much impressed with the Wild Turkey and took some breeding specimens back to Europe. This species was a common game animal in America for the Pilgrims, and later it was nearly driven to extinction by over-hunting. It is now making a strong comeback in many states.

In contrast to the domestic turkey, hunters consider the Wild Turkey a very alert and challenging prey. This bird's contributions to the survival of the early settlers caused Benjamin Franklin to suggest its use as the national symbol. He considered it a far "nobler" bird than the Bald Eagle, which, he noted, steals food from other birds and eats dead animals.

The male turkey has a large tail which it can spread in a fan-shaped display like a peacock. Mature males also have a tuft of modified feathers extending from the breast which is called a "beard." Male turkeys have a spur (a bony protuberance) on the backs of their legs above the toes. Female turkeys are called "hens," young males "jakes," and mature males "gobblers."

Male and Female

Male turkeys have large, fleshy growths on their heads called "caruncles." These growths have a decorative function and become more brightly colored during mating displays. Similar growths are found on other birds. If they appear on top of the head (like on a rooster), they are called "combs." If they hang below the head they are called "wattles."

Gang Wars

Turkey families fight as a group. The dominant male will take on rivals from other families and is backed up by his other brothers. These gangs are called "sib-ship" groups.

Male with "beard"

Males fanning tails in display

White Meat of Turkey

Dark meat is common in the breasts of birds that fly long distances. The dark color is partly caused by the abundant blood vessels needed to sustain long flight. Domestic turkeys, which don't fly, have white breast meat but dark leg meat, due to their constant walking.

Vireos

Red-eyed Vireos

Red-eyed Vireo

The Red-eyed Vireo does indeed have an red eye, but unless the light is from the proper angle and the bird is close, the red eye is not a very useful field mark.

Most vireos sing in the morning or the evening while feeding, but the Red-eyed Vireo sings all day during the breeding season, even on the hottest summer days. It has been observed singing thousands of songs in a single day.

Red-eyed Vireos have always been the most abundant vireos in the Northeast (and perhaps the most noticed, because of their persistent singing), but in recent years all of the vireos seem to be declining in numbers. Many authorities think this is because of the destruction of the tropical rain forests in Central and South America which are their winter homes (except for the White-eyed and Solitary Vireos which winter in the southern U.S).

Yellow-throated Vireo

▷ This is the only vireo in the Northeast with a really bright yellow breast. The yellow breast of the White-eyed is rather pale. Like the White-eyed, the Yellow-throated also wears "spectacles."

Introduction to Vireos

Vireo means "I am green" in Latin. Most of the species of Vireos do have some form of green coloring, usually a dull olive green. Another interesting feature of these small songbirds is the tiny hook at the tips of their upper bills.

Vireos catch insects, but they also eat berries such as those of the wax myrtle and even the fruit of the poison ivy vine. Vireos sing beautiful songs, but they tend to stay hidden in foliage. They are well camouflaged and not as active as many of the other small birds.

Yellow-throated Vireo

Solitary Vireo

MH/Cornell

Solitary Vireo

▷ The Solitary Vireo is noted for its blue-gray crown, white eye-ring, and "spectacles." The bluish cap suggests its former name, Blue-headed Vireo.

White-Eyed Vireo

▷ This is the smallest of the Northeast vireos. Note that in addition to its white eyes, this vireo has yellow markings connecting its eye-rings across the bill, forming a field mark birders call "spectacles."

White-eyed Vireo

MWP/VU

Bird Songs

Many birds have the amazing ability to sing several notes at the same time. This fact was determined using scientific instruments. The simultaneous notes cannot be distinguished by the human ear.

Many bird sounds which are not pleasing to us may be composed of hundreds of rapid notes which seem to be blurred together into a buzz because of our inability to distinguish the individual sounds.

Birds sing to mark territories and attract mates. Their vocal equipment is vastly more sophiscated than our own and they clearly use it to communicate. Only brain power keeps them from developing a full-fledged language.

More Vireos

Two other rather plain-looking vireos not shown in this book can be seen in the Northeast, but neither is very common: the Warbling and Philadelphia Vireos.

Warbling Vireo

This vireo is quite plain with no really distinctive markings. It occurs thoughout the Northeast but is not very common anywhere.

Philadelphia Vireo

The only connection this very plain Vireo has with Philadelphia is the fact that it was first recorded there. It may be the least known of the northeastern vireos. It nests from northern Maine into Canada, so it is only seen in the northeast during migration in the spring and fall. It has a lot more yellow underneath than the Warbling Vireo.

Warblers

Bay-breasted Warbler

The Bay-breasted is known for its chestnut-colored throat and flanks. It is found in spruce and fir habitat. The Bay-breasted is among the first warblers to begin the fall migration, leaving its breeding grounds in New England and Canada as early as the middle of August to begin its journey south.

The Northeast is Warbler Headquarters!

Wood Warblers are found exclusively in the New World (western hemisphere). There are 53 species of Wood Warblers in the United States and Canada, and there are more breeding species in the Northeast (more than 30) than any other part of the country. Upper New York and New England have the highest concentrations of breeding populations. Birders in other parts of the Northeast enjoy viewing warblers in migration as well as their own resident species. Warblers are tiny birds with sharp-pointed bills. Most of them have some areas of yellow coloring. Their food consists largely of insects taken from the crevices of tree trunks, limbs, and leaves, or live insects captured in flight. Many also eat small fruits and berries. Most wood warblers do live in the woods, but not all warble in the sense of singing musical notes. While some species are good singers, others make a variety of sounds including hisses, buzzes, rattles, and whistles. Some warblers sound more like insects than birds. But these sounds are usually distinctive enough to be very useful in identification, especially if the bird is perched high in a tree or hidden by leaves.

The Challenge of Warblers

Because of their beautiful colors and great variety, warblers attract the attention of many birders. Roger Tory Peterson, author of the most famous bird field guide series, calls warblers the "butterflies of the bird world." With their brilliant breeding colors in springtime, they are ideal subjects for beginning birders to test their identification skills.

In the fall, the confusingly subtle colors of autumn plumage, complicated further by the presence of females and immature birds, creates a challenge of birding skills that can lead to a lifetime of study.

Adding further to the challenge is the fact that warblers do not stand still for long periods like shorebirds. There is little time to consult a field guide. A quick look is usually all anyone gets before the bird moves on.

Black-and-White Warbler

The Black-and-White Warbler feeds a little differently from most other warblers. It creeps about on tree limbs and trunks like a nuthatch while looking for insects, and is often seen in upside-down positions. It is among the first warblers to arrive in the Northeast in Spring. Using its strong bill, it digs into tree bark to obtain food which is unavailable to many other birds. While the trees are still bare, it can feed on insects and larvae which lie dormant in the bark.

The broad white stripe above the eye distinguishes it from the Blackpoll, which has a solid black crown.

Blackburnian Warbler

The Blackburnian was named for an English botanist. The name is not a reference to the color of its plumage. Another very appropriate common name is Firethroat. The throat of the male in breeding plumage is a brilliant orange. Blackburnians are difficult to observe because they tend to stay in the tops of tall trees.

Female

Male

Blackpoll Warbler

The Blackpoll Warbler flies farther in migration than any other warbler. Blackpolls winter in South America and their breeding range extends far north. Some Blackpolls must fly from Alaska to Brazil and back each year. Blackpolls from New England migrate over water and fly more than 2,000 miles nonstop to South America.

Blackpolls have very high-pitched songs that may be beyond the hearing range of many birders.

Black-throated Blue Warbler

The male has a combination of colors and patterns possessed by no other warbler. The head and back are dark blue, and the white breast and belly are offset sharply by the black face, throat, and sides.   The white wing patch helps identify this bird even in fall when the trees are filled with migrating birds in non-descript winter plumage. The white wing patch also appears on the female whose coloring is otherwise very different.

Male

Female

Black-throated Green Warbler

The thin, buzzy song of this warbler easily identifies it. The yellow face and the black throat and breast of the male are distinguishing marks. Its back is a kind of olive green, but green coloration is not the most obvious feature of this bird, despite its common name or its Latin species name, *virens*, which means "becoming green." The female completely lacks the black throat and is duller, but note that both male and female have two white wing-bars.

Black-throated Geen Warblers build cup-shaped nests of grasses, moss, hair, and feathers.

Male

Female

Warblers vs Cowbirds

Warblers are among the species most frequently victimized by cowbirds. These "nest parasites" lay their eggs in warbler nests. Which warbler species suffer from these intrusions and why are subjects of current interest to researchers. The response of the warbler parents depends on the species.

Some warblers deal with the problem by removing the cowbird eggs or building a new nest (at a different location or on top of the old nest). However, most warblers succumb to the cowbird scam and raise the cowbird chicks as their own. See page 13 for further details.

Blue-winged Warbler

The Blue-winged Warbler sometimes interbreeds with the closely related Golden-winged. They can produce fertile offspring. There are two hybrid subspecies, Brewster's Warbler and the rarer Lawrence's Warbler.

The more northerly breeding Blue-winged Warbler is continuing to expand its range further into northern New England and New York, chased or pushed by its more southerly competitor, the Golden-winged Warbler.

Warblers

BC/Cornell

Canada Warbler

This warbler is all gray above without wing bars or white in its tail. The short black stripes on its breast have been called a "necklace." It nests throughout the Northeast in wooded swamps with thick undergrowth.

Female

RCS

Male breeding plumage

BS/Vireo

Cape May Warbler

The first specimen was taken in Cape May, New Jersey, although it is only seen there in migration. The Latin species name, *tigrina,* refers to its striping, although the stripes are lengthwise, unlike a tiger's stripes. Note the reddish brown patch of color in the cheeks of the male.

Cape May Warblers are found in spruce trees during summer where, like the Bay-breasted and Nashville Warblers, they capture spruce budworms. During migration, they are often seen in cone-bearing trees.

Male breeding plumage

MWP/VU

Cerulean Warbler

The Cerulean Warbler is a prize sighting for birders in the Northeast because it is a rare bird that is found in mature forests. While in this habitat, it remains in the tops of tall trees, where it is quite hard to see. An important field mark is the narrow, black band across the breast.

Cerulean Warblers build unusual nests which include materials such as lichens and spider silk.

Cerulean means "blue." "Cerulean blue" is one of the traditional hues of the artist's palette.

This warbler is mostly a species of the Midwest, although it reaches southern and western New York and southern New England. It is slowly becoming more common and widespread in the Northeast.

Yellow-breasted Chat

The chat is much larger than any of the other warblers, twice as big as some. It is also the only warbler known to hold food with its foot. An interesting field mark is the white line extending over the bill and around the eyes. Birders call such markings "spectacles."

The chat's song is a highly variable mixture of clucks, whistles, and gurgles that sound more like a mockingbird than a warbler. Because it favors dense thickets and is secretive, it is more often heard than seen. It regularly breeds in the southern portion of the Northeast and but breeds only rarely in northern New York and New England.

Aberrant Warblers

In any classification of birds, there may be one or more species which are a bit different from the others. They are called "aberrant species." A few species of warblers are considered aberrant because they seem so unlike their fellow warblers. For example, the Common Yellowthroat is said to resemble a wren, the Yellow-breasted Chat and the Ovenbird are thrush-like, and the water-thrushes have been compared to sandpipers.

Warblers

Chestnut-sided Warbler

This is the only warbler with an all-white throat, breast, and belly. Note the chestnut-colored stripe for which this warbler is named. It is on its side, just under the wing. The yellow crown is bright in breeding plumage. Male and female are quite similar.

The Chestnut-sided Warbler lives in thickets and brush and is not found where there is a canopy of trees above. It is common on abandoned farms, or in clear-cut forest areas that have become overgrown but do not yet support mature trees.

The scientific name, *pensylvanica*, should have been correctly spelled *pennsylvanica* as it refers to Philadelphia, Pennsylvania, the place where the bird was first observed. However, the misspelling has endured because of an odd quirk in scientific custom. The name given a species by its author traditionally is followed in its exact orginal form, even if it is misspelled!

Connecticut Warbler

Connecticut Warblers are seen in fall migration along the Atlantic coast, but their spring migration is along the Mississippi flyway to their breeding grounds around the Great Lakes and in Canada. They do not breed in the Northeast, but in the fall they fly to the Atlantic coast before beginning their journey south. They walk along the ground like Ovenbirds. Note the gray hood and the white eye-ring.

Feeding High and Feeding Low

Warblers have strong preferences for different levels of habitat. For example, Cerulean and Blackburnian Warblers are usually found in the tops of tall trees. Magnolia and Canada Warblers are found in small trees or bushes. The Ovenbird and the Worm-eating Warbler spend most of their time on the ground. Knowing these habits helps a birder narrow the possibilities when identifying warblers.

82

Golden-winged Warbler

Golden-winged Warbler

This species has been declining in numbers in recent years. It may be that its close relative, the Blue-winged, is more adaptable and is winning in a competition for similar habitat.

The Golden-winged combines a black throat with yellow wing patches.

Hooded Warbler

The black hood of the male Hooded Warbler is like a monk's cowl, covering the top of the head and circling the face. Young females lack the hood or black areas around the face. Older females may have a hood, usually less intense than the male, but in some cases the male and female are quite similar in appearance.

Hooded Warbler

The Hooded Warbler is white on the underside of its tail. It also has whitish outer tail feathers which are conspicuous because it has the habit of fanning its tail.

In the photo at far left, the feathers of the Hooded Warbler are raised as part of a threat display.

Warblers

Kentucky Warbler

The Kentucky Warbler is found in Kentucky and elsewhere in the South, but rarely seen north of Pennsylvania. It nests and feeds on the ground in thick underbrush. Notice the long black streaks below the eyes. Birders call them "sideburns." This warbler also features yellow "spectacles."

Magnolia Warbler

This species also has a misleading name. One of the first specimens recorded was a migrant seen in a Magnolia tree in the South. The name is inappropriate because its usual habitat is a forest of spruce and fir trees. Heavy black stripes over a yellow breast are the main color pattern. Note also the white wing patch. From below, the tail has a black band at the tip, from above, a broad whitish band at the midpoint (see photos at left and below).

Magnolia Warbler
(male in breeding plumage)

△ A pair of immature Magnolia Warblers

84

Mourning Warbler

This bird is so named because of the black on its breast, which is likened to the black crepe of mourning. It is this black patch that distinguishes the Mourning Warbler from the similar Connecticut Warbler.

Nashville Warbler

Mourning Warbler

Nashville Warbler

Nashville Warbler

This bird was named for the place where it was first observed and recorded. The key field marks are the white eye-ring, yellow throat and breast, and gray head. Nashvilles especially like birch and aspen habitats. Although their nests are built on the ground, they forage in the tops of trees.

Orange-crowned Warbler

This little bird is quite dull compared to many other warblers. The touch of orange on its head is only seen when the bird becomes alarmed and ruffs its feathers. The Latin species name, *celata,* means "hidden" and refers to this spot of color. Yellow under the tail and faint streaking on its breast distinguish it from the very similar Tennessee Warbler.

The Orange-crowned is only seen in the Northeast during migration. It does not appear in large numbers, and it may be overlooked, because it frequently travels with flocks of other species of warblers, especially Yellow-rumps. Look for this acrobatic warbler hanging upside down from a small branch.

Orange-crowned Warbler

Ovenbird

The Ovenbird lives on the ground in the forest and depends heavily on camouflage. A female Ovenbird which is incubating eggs often remains motionless until an intruder almost steps on its nest, taking off only at the last second. Ovenbirds (and both species of waterthrush) walk along the ground and do not hop like most other small, perching birds. The famous song of the Ovenbird is described as *"teacher, teacher, teacher."* Note the prominent eye-ring.

△ The name, Ovenbird, refers to its unique nest which is shaped like a Dutch oven with a domed top and side entrance.

△ Look closely for the orange patch on top of the head which is not always visible.

The reddish-brown color on the Palm Warbler's head is intense in the breeding season.

Winter Plumage

Palm Warbler

The name, Palm Warbler, is a misnomer. This species was discovered on a palm-covered Caribbean island and was originally believed to be common to the West Indies. It does winter in the palmetto palms of Florida, but it breeds in the sphagnum bogs of Maine and Canada. The subspecies in the Northeast is the Yellow Palm Warbler.

Tail-wagging Warblers

The habit of some warblers of constantly flicking their tails up and down can be an aid to identification. The Palm Warbler is probably the champion tail-wagger, but two other species also do it frequently (Prairie and Kirtland's).

Northern Parula

This is a bird of the deep woods which is seldom seen. It builds a sack-like nest in the "Old-man's Beard" lichens which hang from trees. If a clump of "moss" appears thick and bulging at the bottom rather than slender and tapered, it may contain a Parula nest.

The name of this species is pronounced in a variety of ways including "PAR-roo-lah," "PAR-you-lah," "pa-ROO-lah," "par-YOU-lah," and even "PEAR-you-lah."

Female

Male

Note the dark breast-band of the male. This warbler is especially active and tends to flick its wings frequently.

Male breeding plumage

Male breeding plumage

Pine Warbler

The Pine Warbler stays high up in tall pine trees and is seldom seen. It was at one time called the Pine-creeping Warbler, as it searches trees for insect eggs and larvae in the same manner as a creeper, but it also captures live insects. It does indeed favor pines and occasionally comes to feeders. Pine Warblers winter in the southern states of the U.S. rather than going to Mexico or Central America like most other warblers.

The Pine Warbler's song is a monotonous succession of staccato notes much like the Chipping Sparrow, but the notes are softer.

Prairie Warbler

"Prairie" is a most inappropriate name for this warbler. It does not live in the grassy plains of the American west but was first discovered in a barren area of Kentucky that was referred to as "prairie" by local residents. Its favorite habitat is low, brushy growth and small, young trees which are not very tall.

The Prairie Warbler has two black marks on its face and streaks on its sides. Note the small, subtle reddish streaks on the upper back of the male.

Prothonotary Warbler

The name "Prothonotary" comes from "Protonotary," an official of the Catholic Church whose function is to keep records of certain acts of the Pope and whose official regalia includes a bright yellow hood. The Latin species name *citrea,* meaning citrus, refers to the color of lemon. The Prothonotary is the only warbler of the Northeast that nests in tree cavities. Its preferred habitat is swampy wooded areas, so it has inspired another common name, Golden Swamp Warbler.

The Prothonotary only nests in a few areas of the Northeast, including western New York, southeastern Pennsylvania, and New Jersey.

American Redstart

This bird has the interesting habit of fanning its tail wide open as it chases insects and flits around like a butterfly. In the Spanish language it is called *candelita,* "small torch," or *mariposa,* "butterfly." The name Redstart refers to an English thrush and reflects the efforts of early ornithologists to place birds discovered in the New World into families known from the Old World. The male has orange patches of color in the wings and tail while females and immature males have yellow patches in the same places.

Male

Female

The famous tail-fanning display

Tennessee Warbler

The Tennessee was first recorded in its namesake state but does not breed there. Its breeding grounds include much of Canada and the Northeast. It can be found among cone-bearing trees as well as deciduous trees. Its population seems to rise and fall with the availability of its favorite food, the spruce budworm.

Male

Immature or Non-Breeding Adult

The Tennessee Warbler spends most of its time in the tops of tall trees, so it often must be identified by its voice alone.

Waterthrushes

The Northern Waterthrush usually builds its nest under the up-thrust roots of trees that have fallen over. It favors water also, but swampy areas rather than fast running streams.

The Louisiana Waterthrush builds a cave-like nest along the banks of a stream. It wades in the shallows and hunts small aquatic creatures.

▷ This bird is the western race of Northern Waterthrush and much whiter than the eastern bird below.

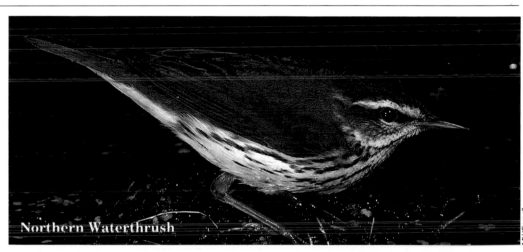
Northern Waterthrush

Louisiana Waterthrush

Northern Waterthrush

Northern-vs-Louisiana

The Louisiana Waterthrush and the Northern Waterthrush are quite similar. When comparing the two species, note the prominent (wider and longer), white eyebrow stripe in the Louisiana, which is yellowish in the Northern. The underparts of the Northern also have a yellowish wash. The throat of the Louisiana is pure white, while the Northern usually has black spots on its white throat.

Wilson's Warbler

This species was named for the ornithologist Alexander Wilson who originally described the bird as Wilson's Black-capped Fly-catching Warbler. It has been likened to a kinglet because it nervously flicks its wings and it is an aerial acrobat in the pursuit of insects. It is most often seen in low thickets around water.

The female Wilson's Warbler is similar to the female Hooded Warbler, but lacks white tail spots. It is also similar to the much more brightly colored Yellow Warbler.

Worm-eating Warbler

This warbler doesn't really eat worms but does eat caterpillars and larvae which may appear worm-like to the casual observer. Its scientific name, *Helmitheros vermivorus*, translates as "Worm-hunting worm-eater."

This warbler is seldom noticed as it feeds while walking along the ground in heavy brush. Its dull, camouflage colors don't help the birder hoping to add it to his list.

Where to See Warblers

Since each warbler species has its own strong preferences for a specific type of habitat, there is no one best place to observe them. However, they are best seen during spring and summer when their breeding plumage is most brilliant and distinctive. They also sing in the spring, which helps with recognition. In fall plumage, they are drab and often difficult to identify.

More about Warblers

Many species of Warblers breed in the northern United States and Canada. The breeding season lasts for about three months. They then spend several months in migration, and about six months wintering in Central and South America. There is a theory that these birds are basically South American species that developed the migratory habit of breeding in North America because it allowed them to escape competition from other local species during this important period.

Whiplash from Warblers

Birders should consider a good insurance policy before going after these birds, because it is easy to strain the neck watching them dash around in the upper branches of trees.

Yellow Warbler

The Yellow is one of the best known warblers because of its wide range and its frequent appearance in home gardens, where it is not shy. It is often called the Yellowbird and sometimes mistaken for an escaped Canary. The Latin species name, *petechia*, derives from a medical term for markings on the skin and is a reference to the prominent rusty streaks on the breast of the male Yellow Warbler.

△ "If my mother fed me that, I'd close my eyes too!"

The black eye of the Yellow Warbler is very prominent in contrast to its pure yellow face.

The Yellow Warbler's song has been translated as "*Sweet, sweet, sweet,*" or "*Weet, weet, weet.*"

Birding Activities

What do birders do in the pursuit of their hobby? Many are "listers." They keep lists of all the species of birds they have personally observed and identified. For some people this is a very competitive activity. There are state lists (birds in one's own state), life lists (a total of all species seen anywhere), North American lists, etc. After all the common and uncommon birds have been sighted, the really competitive part becomes a matter of spotting the rare appearances of birds that are out of their normal range. These birds are called accidentals" or "vagrants."

The birding community is very enthusiastic (some would say

Doonesbury   BY GARRY TRUDEAU

fanatic). The sighting of a rare accidental often excites hundreds of people to board airplanes and travel long distances to add to their lists. This is called "blitzing" among the faithful. Some birders pay a fee to subscribe to a hotline service which alerts them to these opportunities. Really hotshot listers have North American lists of over 600 species. Birders also compete for the most species seen in a year. It helps to be rich because top competitors must fly all over the country and immediately zoom to any place a rare bird has been spotted. The record for a one-year list is 713 species, far more than most birders have on their life lists.

Yellow-rumped Warbler

This bird was formerly called the Myrtle Warbler because of its preference for the fruit of the wax myrtle tree. These fruits are rather wax-like and few other birds can digest them. This special ability makes possible the Yellow-rumped Warbler's early migration north (March and April). The abundant supply of wax myrtle fruit and the similar bayberry fruit keep the species well fed in early spring.

In 1974, taxonomists (those scientists concerned with classification) combined the Myrtle Warbler with a western species, Audubon's Warbler, and both birds then became Yellow-rumped Warblers. Many birders still use the name Myrtle Warbler, which is not entirely incorrect, because "Myrtle" still describes what is now considered the eastern subspecies of the Yellow-rumped Warbler.

The Yellow-rumped frequently gathers in flocks of thirty or forty birds. Its call is described as a "check" sound.

The Yellow-rumped Warbler weaves feathers of other birds into its nest in such a way that the feathers cover the eggs when the female is away. This type of nest is unique among warblers.

Breeding plumage

△ Notice the white throat, and the yellow on the top of the head, flanks, and rump. Uncouth birders call these fellows "butter-butts."

Winter plumage

Common Yellowthroat

The Common Yellowthroat is one of the common warblers in the Northeast. It is found in marshes, swamps, and wet thickets and is easily recognized by its black, "Lone Ranger" face mask. Note the white belly. The female has no mask. Its familiar song is described as *"witchity, witchity, witchity,"* or *"cheeseburger, cheeseburger, cheeseburger."*

The Common Yellowthroat has a huge range. It breeds throughout the entire continental United States, most of Canada, and parts of Alaska. Perhaps because of this wide distribution, a number of races, or subspecies, have developed.

The Common Yellowthroat behaves more like a wren than a warbler. It prefers low shrubs or grassy habitats and often skulks through the underbrush instead of flying.

Yellow-rumped (Winter)

Other Warblers with Yellow Rumps

There are three warblers in the Northeast that have yellow rumps: the Yellow-rumped Warbler, the Magnolia Warbler, and the Cape May Warbler.

The Urge to Migrate

Long before anyone thought to band birds to study their movements, it was obvious that certain birds disappeared in fall and reappeared again in spring. Centuries ago it was believed that birds hibernated during these periods or even flew to the moon! Aristotle speculated that redstarts changed into robins to survive the cold and that swallows buried themselves in mud. It is now known that migration is a seasonal movement between habitats. Approximately three quarters of all North American birds are migratory.

According to one theory, migration got its start when booming populations forced birds to expand their range. Those birds whose timing and sense of direction was fortunate found food and breeding space and were successful in reproducing their kind. Over thousands of years, migratory patterns developed. Birds that arrived late or early or flew off course did not survive and did not reproduce their kind. However, the question of how it all started is quite complex and differs from species to species.

Although many people believe birds migrate to escape cold weather, birds, as a group, are actually quite capable of dealing with cold. The driving force behind

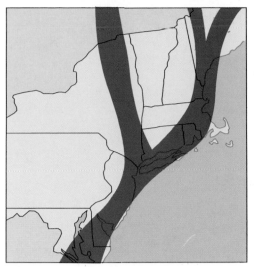

This is the Atlantic Flyway as it is often shown in textbooks, but migration is actually a wider phenomenon occuring over every square inch of the Northeast.

migration seems to be food supply (although the immediate trigger seems to be the changing length of daylight). Some migrations are short, for example from the top of a mountain to the valley below. However, a number of species migrate from one end of the world to the other.

The migration of many species is timed very precisely to the rhythm of insect population surges, seed production of certain plants, etc. Birds such as crows and jays which can eat a variety of foods usually do not migrate because they can adapt their wide ranging diets to the changing seasons.

Some birds have specialized needs. For instance, the Yellow-bellied Sapsucker needs warm sunlight to liquify tree sap and make it flow, so when cold weather comes, it must migrate. But, on the other hand, many woodpeckers need not migrate because they can dig out bugs which have burrowed quite deeply into trees to hibernate.

The riddle of how birds migrate has never been completely solved. It is now believed that they take a variety of navigational clues from the sun, the stars, wind directions, and from many sources that humans cannot sense such as the magnetic field of the earth.

The vast majority of migrating birds are invisible to us, because much of their movement is at night or at too high an altitude to be easily observed. However, radar reports, plus the occasional large kills from the guy wires of tall towers, and unusual weather conditions that force migrating birds to the ground, all paint a picture of awesome numbers, a vast movement of perhaps billions of birds.

What does all this mean to the birdwatcher? A lot! Experienced birders tend to ignore the resident birds they see every day and get very excited during the spring and fall when waves of migrants bring new and interesting species into their areas.

Migrant Traps

Most birds have trouble flying in bad weather. The huge but largely invisible flow of birds through the migration highways of the sky becomes very noticeable and of great interest to birders when bad weather forces large numbers of migrating birds to seek temporary shelter on the ground. When a migrating flock encounters a storm and is forced down, birders call this sudden appearance of thousands of birds a "fallout."

Birds seeking a haven from bad weather follow the maxim "any port in a storm" and head for the nearest likely shelter. For birds flying over New York City, this could be Cen-

tral Park, the only green area in sight for miles. This is called an "oasis" migrant trap. A city park, a clump of trees, a source of water in the mountains, all can become migrant traps when the weather conditions are right. Birds flying over water head for the nearest land when bad weather threatens. This is usually a peninsula or island sticking out into the water such as Cape Cod, Massachusetts, Monhegan Island, Maine, and Block Island, Rhode Island.

Birds often follow narrow stretches of land to avoid flying over water. In the case of Cape May, when the south-bound migrants reach the end of the land,

many species double back to find a less distant crossing. However not all land birds migrate over land. Some species migrate across the Gulf of Mexico, and the Blackpoll Warbler flies from New England to South America nonstop over the Atlantic Ocean.

Central Park

Waxwing

Cedar Waxwing

The Cedar Waxwing's face mask and crest give it very distinctive appearance. Also impressive is the size of waxwing flocks during migration. Waxwings are very social. They migrate in flocks, and also stay together during winter. Waxwings rely heavily on berries, and are important in dispersing seeds. Flocks of waxwings can strip a holly tree in just a few minutes.

Waxwings perform an interesting act of cooperative behaviour. Waxwings sitting on a branch sometimes pass a berry from one bird to another until one finally swallows it.

The name "waxwing" comes from the brilliant red tips of their wing feathers which look like drops of bright red candle wax. They are actually thick deposits of pigments that grow out of the tips of the feather shafts. These colorful blobs, whose function is not known, are unique to waxwings.

Once recognized, the Cedar Waxwing's call, a high pitched "*zeee*" sound, is unmistakable and can be distinguished as large flocks of migrating birds fly overhead.

Woodcock

American Woodcock

The American Woodcock, also known as the "timberdoodle," is sometimes confused with the Snipe. However, it is really quite distinctive if you look closely. They live in different habitats. Woodcocks prefer wooded swamps while Snipes are found in open marshes.

At Moosehorn National Wildlife Refuge near Eastport, Maine, there is a large concentration of woodcocks, but even there they are hard to find, because they stay hidden and are perfectly camouflaged. The complex patterning of the woodcock's plumage makes it very difficult to see in the leaf litter of woodlands.

"Going to town on a Saturday night." An American Woodcock makes a rare visit to civilization.

Woodcocks have amazing peripheral vision. Their somewhat bug-eyed appearance is due to the wide placement of their eyes on the sides of their heads.

Woodcocks start their courtship displays in the chilly weather of early March, much sooner than most other birds. Woodcock courtship is rather spectacular. The male flies hundreds of feet into the air in a spiral and then descends to the ground like a falling leaf while giving a chirping call. These displays are most common at dusk. The call of the woodcock, mostly heard in spring, is a "*peent*," a call very similar in tone to that of the Common Nighthawk.

Eyeshine

Some birds (and some mammals) strongly reflect light which is shined into their eyes at night. This phenomenon is not fully understood. Some birds have special layers of cells in the area of their retinas which might be responsible, but there are other species which also show eyeshine without any such structures. It is known that some birds will freeze and can be closely approached when confronted in the darkness with a beam of bright light.

Woodpeckers

Woodpeckers are very important for the control of wood-boring insects, and their effect is magnified, because after a woodpecker has opened the bark, other birds can also hunt the insects inside. However, improved forestry techniques along with the development of many woodland areas has meant fewer dead trees for nesting and feeding and a decline of woodpecker populations. Competition from starlings for nesting sites has added to the problem.

Woodpeckers have stiff tail feathers which, like those of the Chimney Swift, help to brace the birds as they cling vertically to trees.

Pileated Woodpecker

This is the largest woodpecker in the Northeast. It is almost as big as a crow, but more slender. Its large size and flashy red tuft of feathers on its head mark it as a most impressive bird.

Pileated Woodpeckers are very powerful birds. When they start to chisel, the chips really fly, and not small chips either. The Pileated Woodpecker can reach insect colonies deep inside trees. Partially rotted logs of considerable size can be completely demolished in very little time.

Large cavities are made in trees by Pileated Woodpeckers just for sleeping. The holes are usually oblong rather than round. These are called "bedroom nests." The holes of the nesting cavities used for breeding are usually more roundish in shape.

Female

Some people pronounce the name *PILL-ee-ated* and some pronounce it *PIE-lee-ated*. Both ways are acceptable. It depends on whether you choose to use the Latinized pronunciation or the English pronunciation.

The Pileated Woodpecker is not a common bird but is found throughout the Northeast. It requires extensive forests and a large territory to meet its food requirements.

△ Male and female are very similar, but the female has a black forehead and lacks the small red stripe that extends behind the lower bill (called a moustache by birders).

Red-Headed Woodpecker

Although many woodpeckers have red markings on their heads, this is the only woodpecker whose head is solid red in color. It is seldom seen as far north as New England.

Downy Woodpecker

The Downy is the most common woodpecker in the Northeast and is also the smallest woodpecker in the United State and Canada. It is often seen at suet feeders in winter and makes use of dead trees for its nest. It will circle around a tree trunk to hide.

Female

△ Upside-down downy? This little woodpecker is frequently seen in this position.

▷ The male downy has a small red patch on the back of its head and a long, white patch on its back.

◁ The female looks very much like the male, but does not have the red patch.

Male

Woodpeckers

Northern Flicker

There are three types of flickers in the United States. The race in the west has a reddish color under its wing and tail feathers and is called Red-shafted. The Gilded Woodpecker is the southwestern race. The flicker race found in the Northeast shows bright yellow under the wing and is called Yellow-shafted. All three races are now considered one species, the Northern Flicker.

This woodpecker is often seen on the ground where it hunts for ants. It also eats berries and acorns. It is different from most other woodpeckers because its back is brownish in color rather than having a black and white pattern. When the flicker flies away, it shows a white patch on its rump.

The adult flicker has a red V-shaped marking on the back of its head. The male also has a black stripe extending behind its beak. Birders call it a "moustache." Scientifically, it is called a "malar stripe."

▷ This flicker shows a trace of the yellow-shafted wing feathers. This view also reveals the red V-shaped marking on the back of its head.

△ Flicker on the ground hunting ants.

△ The female is similar to the male, but lacks the black "moustache" marking.

Hairy Woodpecker

This woodpecker looks like a large Downy but has a much longer beak. It is a resident of deep woods, swamps, and old growth pine forests but often comes to suet feeders, especially in winter.

Note that the "hairs" under its beak, from which it get its name, are actually shaggy-looking feathers.

Yellow-bellied Sapsucker

This woodpecker earns its living by drilling many rows of small holes in a tree's trunk, then returning later to lick up the sap that drips from these open wounds in the tree. The insects which become stuck in the sap provide additional food.

Why Do Woodpeckers Pound on Trees?

Beating and chiseling helps woodpeckers find food by removing bark and revealing hidden insects. It enable them to carve nesting cavities. Their pounding also creates a drumbeat rhythm that substitutes for song and will attract a mate or alert other males to a territorial claim. Woodpeckers have been observed drumming when there was no apparent purpose. There is speculation that they sometimes pound away just for the pure joy of the sound, but this has not been proven.

Why Do Woodpeckers Pound on Wooden Houses?

Woodpeckers are usually looking for food or sounding to mark their territories when they pound on houses. It could also be an indication that a building has termites. In one case it was determined that a woodpecker was drilling the side of a house because of the ticking of an alarm clock inside. Woodpeckers often locate insects by sound, so the ticking noise caught the bird's attention.

Woodpeckers

Red-Bellied Woodpecker

This bird is a member of a group of woodpeckers called "ladder-backs," because of the step-by-step black and white pattern on their backs.

In spite of its name, its belly is rather white. If you look closely, there is just a touch of reddish color on its belly. It is sometimes visible if the bird is in just the right position. This reddish patch becomes much more prominent during the breeding season (April to August).

The Red-bellied Woodpecker is sometimes confused with the Red-headed Woodpecker because both have red markings on their heads. But the Red-bellied Woodpecker only has a red stripe on its crown and nape; its head is not entirely red. The Red-headed has a red face while the Red-bellied only has a blush.

A red-bellied woodpecker finally shows his red belly – such as it is.

Red-bellies are primarily southern birds, but in recent years they have been expanding their range northward. They now nest regularly as far north as Connecticut, southern New York, and Massachusetts.

The beautiful "ladder-backed" pattern is prominent on this juvenile Red-bellied Woodpecker, but the distinctive red stripe has not yet developed on its head.

Three-toed Woodpeckers and Black-backed Woodpeckers

The Three-toed and Black-backed Woodpeckers are the only woodpeckers with a yellow patch on their heads. As their name suggests, the Three-toed have three toes instead of the usual four. The ranges of both species are restricted to the coniferous forests of the far north and they only rarely wander into northern New England in winter. Note that the Three-toed has a ladder-back and the Black-backed, a solid black back.

Black-backed Woodpecker (Female)

Black-backed Woodpecker (Male)

Three-toed Woodpecker (Male)

Wrens

Carolina Wren

The Carolina Wren is quite comfortable around man and has the endearing habit of nesting in all kinds of man-made containers, from flower pots to old aprons. Many people have laid down some object, such as an old hat, in a garage and later found they could not use the item until a pair of wrens had finished their nesting season. Wrens are insect-eaters and are regarded as very beneficial to man.

Note the prominent white strip over the eye. The Carolina Wren is common in the mid-Atlantic states but far less common in New England.

Nesting Territories

When it comes to defending a nest, most birds are only worried about their own kind. This is why several different species of birds may nest in the same tree without any problem.

More Details about Breeding

A common feature of many migratory species is that the males arrive in a breeding area first and establish territories. The females arrive a week or so later, and then the males start competing for mates.

In folklore, it is good luck
if a wren builds its nest in a house.

Wrens

Sedge Wren

This shy bird was formerly called the Short-billed Marsh Wren. The male perches in tall grasses to sing and may continue its songs all night. The Sedge Wren does not like habitats that are too wet, and it is more likely to be found in sedge meadows than in reeds and cattails. When disturbed, it disappears among the grasses and is very hard to find.

What Makes a Male Bird Attractive to Females?

For many species, the female's preferences are an important part of mating. It is not completely known what factors female birds consider in choosing mates. It may be that the quality of the male's territory is the main factor. In other words, they marry for money. Male aggressiveness, and a strong, clear song may be important in attracting a female, but, on the other hand, males with the most aggressive behavior also usually have the best territories. Sometimes a female will choose to share a mated male who possesses a fine territory rather than choose an unmated male with a lesser territory.

The Sedge Wren, like the Marsh Wren, has a streaked back. However, the Sedge Wren also has a streaked crown. Compare these markings to those of the Marsh Wren shown below.

Marsh Wren

The Marsh Wren looks much like a Carolina Wren with a white stripe over the eye, but it also has white markings on its back. It is found in cattail marshes and often in brackish or salt marshes. It builds a large nest with a side entrance and suspends it from reeds.

Audubon Did It Too

In many bird books written thirty or forty years ago, there is constant reference to "collecting" specimens, which basically meant killing the birds for further study or for display as mounted specimens.

Today, most ornithologists opt for collecting with a camera, especially with rare species, although a few birds are still collected, with proper government permits, for preparation as museum specimens.

House Wren

The House Wren is common, in its proper habitat, throughout the Northeast. These wrens have been described as "mouse-like" because they often prefer to run through grasses rather than fly. They have a bubbling song full of trills and can often be persuaded to nest in backyard wren-houses. These should have small openings to prevent "hostile takeovers" by swallows or sparrows. House Wrens can usually take care of themselves and can even pose a threat to other species, such as the Bluebird, by piercing unguarded eggs with their sharp beaks.

House Wren

Winter Wren

This is the only wren of the deep woods. It prefers to nest in the stumps of overturned trees. It has a vigorous, bubbling song. The Winter Wren has a very short tail and is darker than other Wrens. Note also the dark bars on its sides which continue around its belly.

Winter Wren

MWP

BIRDS OF PREY

Birds of prey, also known as "raptors" (from a Latin word meaning to rob, seize, and carry off), kill other animals for food. In American Indian cultures, these birds were admired and even worshipped for their hunting skills. The early European settlers saw these same birds occasionally kill domestic animals and viewed them as a threat to their survival. It is theorized that from this history, fear and hatred of birds of prey was passed down through the generations. Certainly, it is felt by some people today. For many rural people, any hawk is a chicken hawk and their first reaction upon seeing such a bird is to reach for a gun. This is true in spite of the fact that all raptors are now protected by law.

It is now known that predators and the prey are dependent upon each other. If predators do not hold populations of prey animals in check, these animals might overpopulate and destroy their food supply, thereby threatening their own survival. If the population of the prey animals declines, so will the population of predators, so a balance of both populations is maintained.

Bald Eagle

The national bird, the Bald Eagle, is threatened, with probably less than 500 pairs remaining in the lower 48 states.

Bald Eagles are not bald. The adult birds (both male and female) have white feathers on their heads. The young birds have dark heads and do not get their white head and tail feathers until they are three to five years old.

◁ Bald Eagles have a spectacular courtship ritual known as a "cartwheel display" in which the male and female eagles grasp each other's talons and tumble over and over through the sky.

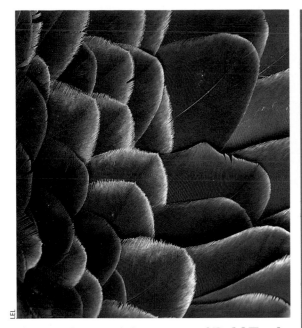

△ The beautiful pattern of Bald Eagle feathers.

▷ The true nature of this "conversation" is anyone's guess. Also open to discussion is the question of which bird is the "husband" and which is the "wife."

The eagle's diet includes a lot of fish and some waterfowl such as coot, moorhen, and ducks as well as mammals such as muskrat, squirrels, and rabbits. Eagles catch fish by grabbing them out of the water with their talons, or by stealing them from Ospreys, but Bald Eagles are also carrion-eaters. The waterfowl they take are mostly sick or injured birds that would not have survived long.

Eagles build huge nests and return to them year after year. The nest shown in the photo above is seven feet wide and 60 feet above the ground.

Before laying eggs, eagles prepare their nest by collecting branches. The branches are used to build a barrier around the edge of the nest. Through such annual additions, eagle nests keep growing in size each year until they are destroyed by storms. Sometimes they survive for many years and become truly huge structures.

△ Immature Bald Eagles are dark in color.

Adult chasing immature from perch

BB

LEL

Bald Eagles have persisted as nesting birds in northern New York and Maine and have been reintroduced into a number of northeastern states. Eagles winter in the northeast and also appear during migration.

Golden Eagle

The Golden Eagle is the Thunderbird, the messenger of the gods revered by American Indians. The adult is all dark, both above and below. Most Golden Eagles in the US are found in the West. It is a thrill for East Coast birders to spot one during migration.

LMS

Hawks

Accipiters are hawks which have short, rounded wings and long tails. Because they eat small birds, they are called "bird hawks." They are distinctive for their pattern of flight which consists of a few wing flaps and then a glide. Female accipiters are noticeably larger than males.

Sharp-shinned Hawk

The Sharp-shinned Hawk derives its name from the fact that its feathers do not extend as far down its legs as other hawks.

Known as a "Sharpie" among birders, this small hawk is responsible for most of the bird kills around backyard feeders in winter. Sharpies find a perch in view of a feeder and wait until small birds appear before striking. With good hunting, a Sharpie may remain near the same feeder for months.

Planting dense shrubbery nearby will provide the birds at the feeder some protective cover. On the other hand, there are some people who would prefer the hawk and would not mind losing a few songbirds to keep him around.

△ The wide-spread tail helps the Sharpie decrease speed for landing and also increases maneuverability when it is chasing prey through forests and dodging trees.
▽ In the photo below, the tail is compressed to a streamlined, narrow strip for rapid flight.

△ Note the small size of the "sharpie." The bird at left is an adult. The bird on the right is an immature.

△ This photo shows the short, rounded wings and long tail that are typical of accipiters. Note also the bare legs (visible in the photo at the top of the page) from which this hawk take its name.

107

Northern Goshawk

The name goshawk comes from "goose-hawk," a reference to one type of prey.

The goshawk is known as an unusually ferocious predator and will not hesitate to attack humans that approach its nest.

For this reason and because the Peregrine Falcon is not abundant, the goshawk has been a popular substitute for those few people in the Northeast who engage in sport falconry.

Note the distinctive white stripe above the goshawk's eye and its elegant plumage.

△ Goshawk guarding a fresh kill.

Cooper's Hawk

The Cooper's Hawk is very similar in appearance to the Sharp-shinned Hawk. It is larger and its tail is rounded rather than square, but it may be impossible to tell the difference by casual observation.

The wing shape of these two hawks is such that they can change direction rapidly and fly through dense woods in pursuit of their prey. Cooper's Hawk pursues mostly songbirds.

Northern Harrier (Marsh Hawk)

The harrier preys on small birds and animals. Its name is derived from "harry," meaning "to plunder." Its habitat is marsh areas and it was formerly called the Marsh Hawk. Since marsh habitat is disappearing, harriers are becoming less common.

Unlike other hawks, harriers hunt by flying close to the ground where they can hear their prey as well as see it, a hunting technique also employed by owls. Harriers are usually seen flying low over open fields in search of rodents.

Second year male (winter)

First year male (winter)

Young Northern Harrier in nest

The Bird that Became an Airplane

An unusual behavior of the Northern Harrier is its tendency to hover over prey before diving to dispatch it. This hovering ability has been duplicated by man in a combat airplane which is able to take off vertically without a runway, then change directions and fly conventionally. This airplane appropriately is called a harrier.

Buteos

Buteos are large, soaring hawks with broad wings and wide tails. They are also known as "buzzard hawks," after their European common name. Their prey consists of mice, rabbits, and other small creatures.

Red-tailed Hawk

The Red-tailed is the most widespread of all the hawks in the United States.

△ Falcons and hawks have notched beaks. The notch is used for extra leverage, like the notch in a pair of wirecutters. It is handy for cutting through tough material such as bone. This feature is called a "tooth-bill."

The red tail of the Red-tailed Hawk is easy to spot even in flight. However, there are many immature Red-tails seen in migration. They do not have this handy field mark but still show the light breast and streaked belly.

△ This view shows the reddish-colored tail feathers which give this bird its name. Only the mature birds have the red tail.

A Red-tailed hawk at its nest with downy chicks. The Red-tailed Hawk has a white breast with a band of streaks across the belly that birders call a "cummerbund," or "belly-band."

Rough-legged Hawk

Rough-legged hawks have different color phases ranging from light to dark. Notice the feathers extending down the legs which give it its name. Although the lighter Rough-legged Hawks show a dark belly band, Red-tails in winter also have this feature, so the feathering on the legs becomes important for identification. Note the white tail crossed with a black band which can be used for indentification in all color phases.

The Rough-legged breeds in the far north and only ventures into the Northeast in winter to seek food when rodent populations in Canada decline. Its habits and range are similar to those of the Snowy Owl. It is often seen hovering while searching for prey. Rough-legged Hawks are most commonly seen in winter in the marshes bordering the Northeast coastline.

Light phase

Dark phase

Rough-legged Hawks have color phases: light and dark. Note that the light phase bird in the photo above has dark feathers crossing its midsection which birders call a cummerbund or belly band.

Much color variation is possible, however, the underside of the tail of the Rough-legged Hawk remains white, crossed with a dark band.

This photo shows in detail the feathering of the legs for which the Rough-legged Hawk is named.

Built-in Goggles

The nictitating layer is a transparent membrane located under a bird's eyelid. It can be drawn across the eye (horizontally). Its function is to protect the eye during flight like a pair of goggles. It prevents fast-moving air from drying the eye.

Red-shouldered Hawk

Note the patch of reddish color on the shoulder. These hawks are found in wet areas near streams and swamps unlike the Red-tailed Hawk which prefers drier woodlands.

Red-shouldered Hawks found in the South are quite pale in color compared to those found in the Northeast.

The Red-shouldered Hawk has a very interesting courtship display. A pair of Red-shouldered Hawks rolls over on their backs during flight and may even fly upside down for a short distance. They are known to decorate their nests with fresh green leaves.

▽ This Red-shouldered Hawk is trying to entice the snake to strike at its upraised wing. It would then have a chance to grab the snake.

Broad-winged Hawk

The Broad-winged is a small hawk which is about the size of a crow. Along with the Red-tailed, it is one of the most common hawks. This species is exciting to hawk-watchers because it is the only northeastern hawk that migrates in flocks and these "freight trains" of birds sometimes number a hundred or more. On the biggest day, more than 10,000 were recorded passing an observation point and were said to have stretched from horizon to horizon. In flight, the black and white tail bands (which are of equal width) are important field marks.

The Broad-winged is considerably less shy of humans than other hawks and will often allow a close approach.

Immature

Adult

Forbidden Birds of the Bible

Of the 20 birds that the Israelites were forbidden to eat, most were birds of prey. One of the reasons these birds were considered unclean was that they ate flesh and blood. The eating of blood was forbidden as blood was regarded as the essence of life (when blood flowed out of the body, an animal or human would die). Hence, to eat blood was an offense against God (Leviticus 17: 13-14). Among the birds of the Northeast included on the forbidden list were the eagle, osprey, vulture, nighthawk, owl, hawk, swan, cormorant, heron, and cuckoo.

Looking at it another way, these birds may have been the beneficiaries of the first list of protected species in recorded history. However, these restrictions were later lifted for the followers of Christ after Peter experienced a vision (Acts 10: 9-13). Nowadays, Christians are more likely to consider the words of Jesus "Not what goes into the mouth defiles a man, but what comes out of the mouth, this defiles a man."

The Audubon Christmas Bird Count

Audubon clubs across the nation select one day during the Christmas season and club members spend all 24 hours of that day systematically counting the birds in their area (within a 15 mile diameter). The idea originated in the late 1800's as a contest to see who could shoot the most birds in one day, but in 1900, Frank Chapman of the American Museum of Natural History had the notion of civilizing the sport by making it a visual count of birds rather than a hunt. Since then the Christmas bird count (CBC) has taken on scientific importance. The statistics from the count are compiled to give researchers information about changing bird populations.

Hawkwatchers at the north lookout of Hawk Mountain

Hawkwatching

Migrating hawks follow clearly defined routes and can be observed at a number of places where these routes narrow and concentrate tens of thousands of birds. Two legendary observation points are Hawk Mountain in Pennsylvania where birders observe migration along mountain ridges and Cape May, New Jersey, the ideal spot to view hawks migrating along the coast.

On bright, clear days at Hawk Mountain, species such as the Broadwinged Hawk soar in the thermals created by rising warm air currents. Large numbers are sometimes seen circling in the updrafts. These swirls of hawks are called "kettles."

On windy days, the ridge-riding species are prevalent. The Red-tailed Hawk makes use of the updrafts created as wind blows up the sides of ridges. Red-tails can be seen sailing along the crests of the hilltops.

The pilots of gliders and sailplanes have followed the same routes taken by hawks and have achieved some very long-distance flights by using the same techniques as these masters of the air.

Cape May, New Jersey

On the shady north side of the ridge, hawks ride the updrafts created by the prevailing northerly winds.

A "kettle" of hawks soars upwards in a thermal, taking advantage of the lift as the warm air rises. After being pushed to a higher altitude, the hawks glide to the next thermal.

This drawing explains the photo at left. The migrating hawks travel down both sides of the ridge shown in the center of the photo and often pass directly over the observers, almost at eye level.

Sunlight heats the south side of the ridge creating warm, rising air currents called "thermals."

Birders in the Northeast are fortunate in having most of the best hawk lookouts in the country, although there is speculation that new sites may still be discovered in the West. Hawks usually follow mountain ridges or coastlines in their migrations and the geography of the Northeast has created a number of excellent concentration points.

Hawkwatchers are enthusiastic people who are willing to accept a feast or famine of birds as changing weather triggers migratory movement. The devotees study weather patterns in hopes of predicting and being present during one of the fabled "Big Days" when as many as five to ten thousand hawks pass an observation point. The really big movements of birds are in the fall and usually occur a few days after the passage of a cold front.

Hawkwatching treks to mountain lookouts are most rewarding in September and November. During spring migration (which peaks in April) the flow of birds is much more widespread. The hawks are not as concentrated at the traditional observation points as they are during the fall migration.

Expert hawkwatchers scan the horizon with binoculars and pick up incoming hawks when they are just tiny specks. Birds of prey appear to be swimming through the air when their flight is observed at a distance. Long before details such as color and field marks become visible, experts make identifications based upon silhouette shapes and also flight styles, the proportion of time spent flapping to the time spent gliding as well as the rhythm.

Another useful clue is the position in which a bird holds its wings when gliding. Some raptors tilt their wings upward, some hold them almost level and some even point their wing-tips downward.

These special identification techniques are necessary for hawks because hawk plumage is much more variable than that of other birds. Also, many of the migrating birds are immatures which lack the clear field marks of adults and whose plumages are confusingly similar.

Each hawk species has its own peak migratory period and it is different at each observation point. For example, the peak for Broadwings traditionally occurs around September 16th or 17th at Hawk Mountain, Pennsylvania, but a week or so earlier at the more northern lookouts. Hawk migration is a constant cycle and there are at least some hawks in migration almost every month of the year. The last Red-tails pass through the Northeast on their way south in late December, and by January the Turkey Vultures are already starting their return journey north.

Hawk Mountain used to be the meeting place for a gun club whose members considered hawks to be nothing more than pests and easy targets. Each year huge numbers were slaughtered just for sport. Fortunately, the property was purchased by environmentalists who created a sanctuary now enjoyed by birders from all over the world.

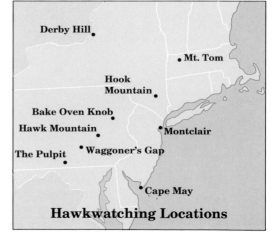

Derby Hill

Mt. Tom

Hook Mountain

Bake Oven Knob
Hawk Mountain

Montclair

The Pulpit   Waggoner's Gap

Cape May

Hawkwatching Locations

Falcons

American Kestrel

Kestrels used to be called "sparrow hawks," but this name is not really appropriate because the kestrel feeds primarily on insects, mice and small lizards and snakes. It is usually seen in the open countryside perched on the limb of a tree and is frequently seen on phone wires, tipping its tail.

Wings are pointed

Males have blue-gray wings

Back and tail are reddish

"Eyes" in the Back of its Head

The kestrel has two spots on the back of its head. It is theorized that, from a distance, these spots resemble eyes. They may help prevent attacks from the rear by larger raptors by giving the illusion that the kestrel is facing the attacker and therefore less likely to be taken by surprise.

Peregrine Falcon

The Peregrine Falcon nearly became extinct in eastern North America as it suffered the harsh effects of pesticides in the environment. Thanks to the efforts of the Cornell University Laboratory of Ornithology, a captive breeding program was organized to produce Peregrines for release in the wild. This prevented disaster and began to restore Peregrine populations after the pesticide problem was brought under control.

For centuries, the Peregrine Falcon has been used by the Arabs along the Persian Gulf to hunt for food and even today, falconry is still very popular in that region as a sport. Top quality birds captured in the wild (so that they do not have to be taught to hunt) can bring prices up to $100,000. This means that smuggling birds can be as profitable as smuggling drugs. It has put extra pressure on the Peregrine Falcon populations in spite of law enforcement efforts.

The Peregrine Falcon dives on its prey at enormous speeds variously estimated from 100 miles per hour to almost twice that speed. A Peregrine Falcon kills its prey by striking it hard with a foot balled-up like a fist or by raking it with sharp talons.

The Peregrine Falcon usually nests on rocky cliffs, often overlooking water, but a large proportion of the Peregrines seen in the Northeast today were raised on buildings and bridges. In winter, Peregrines frequently hunt along the beaches and mud flats where potential prey such as shorebirds and waterfowl congregate.

Peregrine Falcon

△ Elaborate headgear used in sport falconry.

△ Peregrine Falcon showing the pointed wings that are typical of falcons.

▷ Female Merlins are brown in color.

Sport falconry exists in this country, but there are not many practitioners. It takes a great deal of effort. The trainer and the bird must work together daily.

Merlin

The Merlin is midway in size between the tiny American Kestrel and the much larger Peregrine Falcon. The male Merlin has gray-colored wings like the Peregrine Falcon. Formerly, the Merlin was known as the Pigeon Hawk.

Owls

In the United States and much of the western world, the owl is considered a symbol of wisdom and knowledge. The Greek goddess of knowledge, Athena, was often depicted with an owl on her shoulder. However, in many other parts of the world the owl is regarded with fear as an omen of death and disaster. Most likely, this feeling comes from the fact that owls are birds of the night, and darkness is always scary. Their frightening shrieks and moans don't do much to dispel this negative image.

Despite the old superstitions, owls are of great interest to most bird lovers. Even among collectors of wildlife art, owls are extremely popular subjects.

Great Horned Owl

The Great Horned Owl is instantly recognized by its large ear tufts and is familiar to most people because it is frequently cast in TV and movie episodes. Since it is found throughout North America, it is appropriate for just about any setting. Its *"Hoo, hoo"* call is also familiar from the soundtracks of many dramas. The large size of this owl enables it to consume a wide variety of prey, from shrews and mice to rabbits, squirrels, opossums, and skunks.

The Great Horned Owl occupies woodland areas, the same habitat as that of the Red-tailed Hawk. The two birds do not conflict with each other, because the hawk hunts by day and the owl by night.

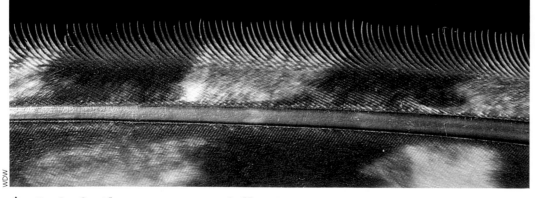

△ Owl feathers are specially adapted so that owls can fly silently and approach their prey without warning. The leading edge of an owl feather is unlike that of any other bird. The feather's edge is soft and downy, which eliminates the usual flapping noise produced by most birds in flight.

Threat display of immature Great Horned Owl

The Great Horned Owl is by far the largest and most powerful resident owl of the Northeast region. Although the Great Gray Owl is larger, it is a rare winter visitor from Canada.

△ An owl can greatly increase its apparent size by raising its wings. Such a display may help to intimidate an opponent such as a hawk.

◁ Great Horned Owls visiting from the northern tundra areas have whitish plumage which matches their snowy environment.

The Remarkable Owls

Owls have remarkable abilities which enable them to hunt in the dark. Their huge eyes allow them to see when other creatures cannot. The position of their eyes on the front of their heads gives them better binocular vision than many other birds whose eyes are on the sides of their heads. How- ever, moonlight and starlight are not constant, so most owls hunt by sound. It is their keen sense of hearing that usually enables them to discover their prey. That is why rodents, which rustle leaves as they run around at night, are among the owl's favorite targets.

Owls

Barn Owl

This owl cannot be mistaken because of its heart-shaped face. It is sometimes called the "monkey-faced" owl. The Barn Owl hunts mammals and is well respected by farmers for helping to control mice and rats.

The Barn Owl belongs to a different family than the other owls in the Northeast. One difference is that the middle claw of the Barn Owl has a serrated, comb-like edge which is used for smoothing feathers.

The Barn Owl is found in almost every country of the world except the very cold northern countries. It is far more widespread than any other owl of the Northeast, but it is uncommon in much of northern New England. As its name implies, it likes to nest in man-made structures and is especially fond of barns and church steeples. The Barn Owl dines on small animals, especially rodents.

The Barn Owl does not "hoot," but has a rasping screech. It has been suggested that this is the owl that should have been named "screech owl."

Great Gray Owl

The Great Gray is the largest owl in North America. Most live in Alaska and remote areas of northwest Canada, but some wander into New England every winter. They are quite tame, perhaps because of their lack of contact with humans.

Note the huge head with the concentric circles around the eyes.

120

Barred Owl

The Barred Owl is recognized by the pattern of bars running horizontally across its chest and the contrasting streaks running vertically down its belly. Notice also the soft, dark-brown eyes. Most of the other owls have eyes which are bright yellow.

The Barred Owl has a strong voice and is the owl most commonly heard at night in residential areas where there are plenty of trees. Its song is the typical "hoot" that most people associate with owls, although many owl species make sounds which are not so loud nor so easy to recognize. The sequence is rhythmic and sounds like *Who cooks for you, who cooks for you?* This vocal pattern is the reason the Barred Owl is also called the Eight-hooter.

Immature

"Do Owls Bring Bad Luck?"

In western culture, the Romans may have started this negative thinking. The Roman emperor Augustus supposedly died after the hooting of an owl predicted his fate. A verse from Shakespeare's "Macbeth" follows the same idea: "It was the owl that shrieked, the fatal bellman which gives the sternest goodnight."

Pellets

Owls, like many birds of prey, spit up balls of indigestible material such as hair, bones, feathers, and claws of their prey. These materials are compressed and rolled into pellets by their digestive system and regurgitated. Inspection of these pellets yields valuable information about the diet of the birds.

△ Note the pattern of white markings on the back.

121

Long-eared Owl

The Long-eared and Short-eared Owls are as different as night and day. The Long-eared Owl hunts only at night and is a bird of the forest while the Short-eared Owl may hunt by day over open fields, salt marshes, and sometimes even beaches.

Immature

The Long-eared Owl has especially long ear tufts which are feathers, not ears, and which are more accurately called "display tufts." Note the deep "V" of feathers between the eyes. The ear tufts are set much closer together than those of the Great Horned Owl.

Long-eared Owls roost during the day close to the tree trunks where their plumage blends with the bark of the tree.

Short-eared Owl

The Short-eared Owl has ear tufts, but, true to its name, they are small (less than an inch in length) and may not be noticed. Although its ear tufts are small, the ears themselves are large and very sensitive. Note also the dark plumage around the eyes.

Short-eared Owls often roost together in groups in winter. There may be dozens of birds huddled together at a roost at those times when they are not hunting.

Both Short-eared and Long-eared Owls put on broken wing and wounded bird acts to draw predators away from their nests. Although common in shorebirds, this behavior is unusual among birds of prey.

Saw-whet Owl

The Saw-whet Owl is tiny, no larger than the average songbird, although it has a large head and fluffy feathers that give it a larger appearance. It is the smallest bird of prey in the Northeast and is often described as "fist-sized". However, it is a very accomplished hunter. It can kill prey larger than itself, such as squirrels, but mice are its favorite food.

The name, Saw-whet, comes from its creaky voice, which is said to resemble the sound of a saw being sharpened on a whetstone. The song for which it is named is rarely heard. More often, it makes a series of toots.

The Saw-whet Owl is seldom seen in the daytime since it hunts at night and hides among thick branches during the day. It is sometimes seen during severe weather when it is forced to scavenge for food in populated areas.

The Saw-whet Owl is known for its amazing tameness. Ordinarily, it will not move from its perch even when a birder stands directly beneath it, and there are stories of birders capturing Saw-whets with their hands.

Adult

Immature

Rules of Listing

Birders are known to be competitive in compiling their life lists. According to the rules of the sport, a bird can be identified by sight or sound, but the bird must be alive. The following story illustrates how eager bird listers can be. A group of birders in New England had called it a day shortly after dark when an unusual owl flew into their car headlights and was injured. As the dying owl was held in the hands of one of the group, his companions gathered around, each guessing an identification before the bird died, so that it could eventually be added to the list once the ID was confirmed. The ID had to be made before the bird expired or it could not be counted. If any of the identifications turned out to be correct, each member of the group could add the bird to his list. In this case the bird was, in fact, a rare Boreal Owl, a prized addition to the list of a New England birder.

Snowy Owl

Unlike most owls, the Snowy can hunt during either the day or night. This ability is essential in the northern part of its normal range, within the Arctic circle, where the sun may remain above the horizon for months.

Note the round head, the small beak which is almost entirely covered with feathers, and the "booted" feet, also covered with feathers.

△ In the Northeast, the Snowy Owl is frequently seen on coastal marshes and beaches. It is a bird of the tundra and is drawn to open flat areas.

Snowy Owl Irruptions

Volcanoes erupt, but Snowy Owls irrupt; that is, they suddenly expand their range. On an average four-year cycle, the Snowy Owl moves from its usual range in Canada to appear in the New England states in increased numbers during the winter. These movements have also been called "invasions." The irruptions of the Snowy Owls follow the rise and fall of rodent populations in Canada.

Pure white form (adult male)

Heavily barred form (immature)

Light or Dark?

The Snowy Owl is an all-white bird, but individual Snowy Owls have different amounts of dark barring in their plumage. The really pure white specimens are usually adult males while immature females may be so heavily barred as to appear all dark. Also, the Snowy Owls from the far north are generally whiter than their relatives living farther south.

Eastern Screech-Owl

The Eastern Screech-Owl is one of the smallest owls. The little screecher has "ear tufts," extra long bunches of feathers on both sides of the head. They are merely for show and do not aid the real ears, which are simply small openings hidden under the feathers. If you see a small owl and it has ear tufts, it must be a screech owl. The Great Horned Owl also has ear tufts, but it is a much larger bird.

The screech-owl usually does not screech but makes a soft, mournful sound. It is capable of a blood-curdling scream, but the scream is rarely heard. It captures all kinds of small prey.

Gray phase

Red phase

◁ The screech-owl has two color phases: gray and red. This variation may occur in the same brood. According to one theory, if screech-owls are living in various habitats, a variety of colors ensures that at least some of the birds will be well matched to their surroundings for camouflage. This may give the screech-owls, as a group, an advantage for survival.

125

Vultures

Vultures are scavengers. They eat dead animals almost exclusively, although they will sometimes feed on garbage. It would be quite rare for a vulture to kill a healthy animal, but they do get impatient and will move in to dispatch an animal that is very sick or dying. Since the removal of the last California Condor from the wild (for a captive breeding program), there are only two vulture species remaining in North America.

Vultures are often mistakenly called buzzards. "Buzzard" is actually a European term for soaring hawks. Many common hawks, such as the Red-shouldered Hawk, are members of this family of "buzzard hawks," also known as buteos.

Turkey Vulture

Birders sometimes call Turkey Vultures "TV's" for short. Turkey Vultures often dine on the squashed animals they find along highways, so, naturally, these delicacies are called "TV dinners."

Turkey Vultures are so named because their bare red heads somewhat resemble the wattles of the Wild Turkey. Whereas a Bald Eagle has feathers on its head, a Turkey Vulture is truly bald. Bare skin is probably easier to keep clean than feathers after eating carrion.

Turkey Vultures are easily recognized in flight even at great distances from the manner in which their wings are held in a V-angle and also the fact that their flight feathers are lighter in color than their wing linings. The Turkey Vulture's see-saw tipping of its wings during flight is often sufficient for identification.

A Clothespin on the Nose

Because of their grisly daily contact with dead animals, many people assume that vultures must have no sense of smell. However, experiments have shown that Turkey Vultures have a very keen sense of smell. They were able to locate dead animals from the air even though the carcasses were covered to prevent visual sighting.

The Skunks of the Bird World

Vultures have a unique defense mechanism. They vomit on would-be predators, and their vomit is said to be so foul smelling as to spoil the appetites of their assailants.

Turkey Vultures roost together in groups, especially in the bare branches of dead trees. They leave their perches in the morning, but not as early as most other birds.

Young Turkey Vultures have black heads and may be mistaken for Black Vultures. In addition to the differences in flight styles described on the previous page, the Turkey Vulture has feathers at the tips of its wings which are lighter in color. Also, the Black Vulture in flight shows a shorter, wider tail than the Turkey Vulture.

Black Vulture

The Black Vulture is quite similar to the Turkey Vulture in its habits, and the two birds often share the same roosts. As the Black Vulture is less bouyant in the air, it is more confined to southern states where it can ride the thermal air currents which are more abundant in warm climates. It appears only as far north as southern Pennsylvania, whereas the Turkey Vulture, a stronger flier, ranges farther north into New England.

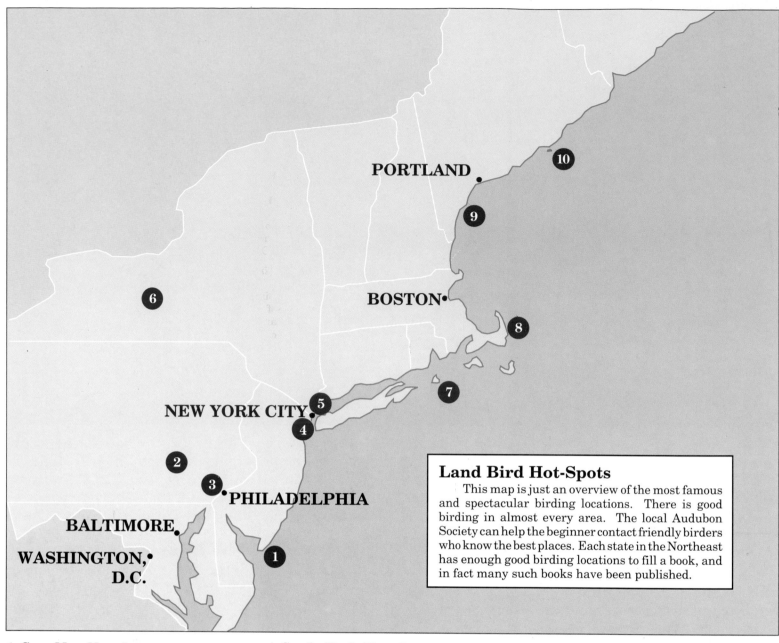

Land Bird Hot-Spots

This map is just an overview of the most famous and spectacular birding locations. There is good birding in almost every area. The local Audubon Society can help the beginner contact friendly birders who know the best places. Each state in the Northeast has enough good birding locations to fill a book, and in fact many such books have been published.

1. Cape May, New Jersey

Because it is located at the tip of a funnel-shaped peninsula which concentrates the flow of migrating birds, Cape May is one of the premier birding spots in the world. It is a mecca for hawk watchers (see pages 114-115). It includes an impressive visitor's center with naturalists available, and a wide variety of habitats nearby. While Cape May is good anytime of the year, the peak of the fall landbird migration is usually September 15th to 25th.

The big days are dependent upon weather conditions. More species have been sighted at Cape May than anywhere else in the US (except Texas, where tropical vagrants occasionally appear). An added attraction is that visitors may witness the migration of the monarch butterfly. (609-884-2159)

2. Hawk Mountain, Pennsylvania

See pages 114-115. Because of the elevation of its lookouts, hawks can sometimes be seen at eye-level. There is an impressive nature center with naturalist guides. The large sanctuary is good for other land birds in addition to hawks. It is located about one half hour west of Allentown. (215-756-6961)

3. Rittenhouse Square, Philadelphia

This is another spot of green in a big city which acts as a lure for migrating birds and concentrates them when conditions are right.

4. Sandy Hook, New Jersey

Sandy Hook is an undeveloped piece of land in an urban sea which acts as an "oasis" trap for migrating birds passing over New York City and New Jersey. It is better in spring than fall.

5. Central Park, New York City

A big city "oasis" which attracts many migrants especially birds which have flown all night and at dawn find themselves over the concrete jungle.

6. Cornell Lab of Ornithology, Ithaca, NY

The Sapsucker Woods Sanctuary features a visitor's center and a bird observatory with a sound system which brings bird calls inside large plate glass windows that shield the birds from the sounds of human observers inside. There are exhibits, a bookstore, and miles of nature trails through various habitats.

7. Block Island, Rhode Island

Columbus Day weekend is the peak of the migration season here and many birding tours are scheduled for these few days. The lure of Block Island is the potential for seeing unusual birds out of their normal ranges. Islands and peninsulas tend to gather birds that are off course. At Block Island and many other points along the coast, birds that are migrating along the coast at night are sometimes pushed out over the water by strong northwest winds. When the sun rises, many head for the nearest shore and land on the island. Most abundant are warblers, creepers, sparrows, juncos, flickers and kinglets.

8. Cape Cod

The peninsula offers a spectacular mix of upland and beach habitats.

9. Biddeford Pool, Maine

Located north of Kennebunkport, this is a migrant trap which is good for warblers and rarities in spring and fall. In this amazing place, lucky birders have even spotted South American species such as the Variegated and Fork-tailed Flycatchers.

10. Mount Desert Island, Maine

The name, Mount Desert, is pronounced both like the sweet stuff and the hot, dry place, but the island probably owes its name to the fact that many sailors deserted their ships here. The main attraction for birders is Acadia National Park. Mount Desert has more breeding warbler species than any other place in the United States. Bald Eagles are common. It is a good place to watch the warbler migration in spring and fall and also great for sparrows and flycatchers. Among the many habitats are the fascinating wet bogs. Rubber boots are helpful for exploration.